Profound Insights

from

Animals and Nature

by

Cynthia Attar

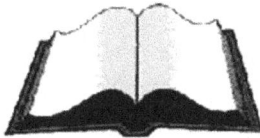

CCB Publishing
British Columbia, Canada

Profound Insights from Animals and Nature

Library and Archives Canada Cataloguing in Publication
Attar, Cynthia
Profound Insights from Animals and Nature / by Cynthia Attar – 2nd ed.
Includes index
ISBN 978-1-927360-93-4
Additional cataloguing data available from Library and Archives Canada

Cover design by Raquel Cuellar: www.raquelcuellar.com
Cover illustration courtesy of www.colourbox.com
Illustrations within book courtesy of www.clipart.com

Address all inquiries to:
Cynthia Attar
28500 Hwy 24
Sunnyside, WA 98944

Publisher: CCB Publishing
               British Columbia, Canada
               www.ccbpublishing.com

Thank You

A grand thank you to all the energetic contributors for this book
and their profound insights of wisdom.
Thank you to all the readers who have the courage to hear
what the wise beings around us have to say.

Dedication

This book is lovingly dedicated to all people
who desire to further their sense of connection, unity, and oneness.

Books by Cynthia Attar

The Mule Companion: A Guide to Understanding the Mule

Profound Writings from Everyday People

Profound Insights from Animals and Nature

Profound Do-it-Yourself Healing with Pet Healing Case Studies

CONTENTS

INTRODUCTION

Congratulations for picking up this book. This tells me you are a highly evolved being with a special love for animals and nature. You have the courage to venture into uncharted waters, the curiosity to delve into unfamiliar territory, and a mindful openness of what is possible. Welcome, it is nice to be in familiar company!

Here's a brief overlay of how this book came to be. As a horse and mule trainer for many years, I was told over and over that I achieved greater results with equines than most other trainers. For some reason I seemed to understand these critters better than other trainers. I didn't think I was doing anything unusual, I just was able to view things through the equine's eyes a bit clearer than some. I wanted more insight, however, so I studied famous and infamous horse trainers who truly seemed to understand equine behaviors and their meaning. Although fascinating and informative, there still was something missing. Other than the animal simply complying with the owner's wishes, I wanted to know if the equine wanted to jump those fences, pull that cart, or cut cows out of a herd. I wanted to know where physically they were hurting, and possibly past events which may be interfering in today's training successes. That would have been wonderful, I thought, but highly unlikely to accomplish.

During my inner spiritual development days I happened upon a book, Kinship with All Life by J. Allen Boone[1]. Boone was a type of Dr. Doolittle who was able to hear directly from the animals what they were thinking, in a telepathic sort of way. (I highly recommend this book.) This communication level was the training link that I was missing. If I could truly hear what the equine was thinking, I would then know how to help him best and get the most out of him at each moment. There was only one problem—I didn't have the natural gift of telepathically communicating with animals. Yet, in what I was reading in Kinship, Boone stated that this communication level was not exclusively a skill for the psychically gifted. Boone suggested that this ability was attainable through study and practice by most anyone who desired.

This was new information at the time, so I began a search. Occasionally I would find others who claimed to tune into animals in this same unusual way. Most of these people were convinced that anyone who desired to do so could tune into their pet's non-verbal voice, and they didn't have to be psychically "gifted." Well, I certainly desired to do this work, so I sought out classes that were offered by accomplished animal communicators. I attended all that I could find and afford. Hey, if it was possible that "psychic-ness" could be taught, I wanted to be that success story. So I set that as my goal.

After a few years of classes and practice, I still felt I wasn't good enough to be a true animal communicator. I worked diligently and did everything the instructors told me. It seemed the information I picked up from animals was really interesting, but I wasn't picking up those "make a believer out of the skeptic" pictures that the real communicators were getting. No matter how hard I tried to see Fifi's mental picture of her food dish, or the color of the bow she wore yesterday, it just didn't happen. Each time I'd come across a picture or words that could be proven wrong, I simply would dismiss it or block it out. During instructed telepathic communication homework, I was getting excited about the content of the words of insightful wisdom from the animals—or maybe it was from my own imagination. Sometimes, the messages surprised me or made me laugh out loud. It sure didn't seem that this information could be coming from me, so maybe they actually were from the animals. Many of those surprising messages were on the verge of being profound insights from the animals. They would tell me things like they were here as models of how we humans can be happy. They said they wanted to

---

[1] J. Allen Boone. Kinship with All Life. Harper. San Francisco, CA. 1954

2

help us humans to evolve, grow, and become more aware of the oneness of all things.

Even with the fabulous information I was getting, it didn't meet the homework criteria. The dog didn't tell me what his house looked like or reveal information that proves to the owner I was really tapping into their pet's mind. So, again, I dismissed the possibility that the words were real, and figured I was making it all up in my mind.

I really dislike not reaching my pre-set goals. I had invested a lot of money and time to accomplishing this telepathic communication level. I was getting some great insights, but I wasn't successful at what the instructors were trying to teach me. What was I to do, just give up the telepathic communication quest and accept defeat? I was in a dilemma.

Just before I scrapped the entire telepathic animal communication dream, I sat down and analyzed the path I had embarked on. I remember thinking to myself, "I wonder if what I do get is good enough. Maybe I'm not supposed to see food dishes, bow colors, or dog houses. Maybe I'm supposed to get higher messages from the animals. Maybe the juicy stuff that I've been getting has been from the animals all along." It was at that point I decided I would continue to dive into the thoughts I was getting from somewhere *and see what the true quality and depth of it could be. I gave up trying to figure out if it really was from the animals or from my own mind. This was just an experiment anyway, it didn't matter much.*

That decision was the birth of this book. I then began to document nearly every chat I had. Many of the chats were shocking, some humorous, and nearly always were they filled with insightful wisdom. This book unfolded beautifully, despite the insecure cloud that followed over my head during these chats.

A few years later I was shocked to realize that I actually have been somewhat psychic all my life but I didn't know it! I learned that I am empathic and telepathic. That means that I feel other's feelings inside my stomach and hear their thoughts in my head. My upbringing was such that this ability was squelched within me and I was told in no uncertain terms that any thoughts I had or feelings I felt were strictly my own—no one else's. As a youngster, my belief from hence forward was that I was incapable of hearing/feeling anyone else. This belief prevented me from doing that telepathic homework and obtaining information from the animals that could be proven or disproven. This personal realization allowed me to further understand that I probably have always heard and felt the horses and mules in training. But since my conscious mind would not believe I could communicate with them telepathically, I would simply react to the equine's thoughts and emotions instinctively—on a subconscious level. It explained that this was how I seemed to understand the horses so well, and got more out of them when training. My desire to be a more insightful equine trainer was finally reached. Since then I have enjoyed my relationships with all animals immensely.

This book is a compilation of the most interesting chats I've had with various beings of this earth. These chats were initially from my own household and farm pets. I then opened up more possibilities and the conversations spread to include wild animals, birds, fish, insects, and such. One day it occurred to me that other aspects of nature such as rivers, wind, moon, and trees may have their own insights about life also. Finally, I added some of the best discussions that I've had with Jessup, a spiritual guide from "upstairs", a term to suggest that which is above or somehow higher than the conscious mind as we know it today. The messages are pretty straight forward, easily understood, with valuable information the reader can relate to and use in their own lives. Are these profound insights from animals and nature, or a figment of my imagination? That is for you to decide. No matter where it has come from, the wise insights between the covers of this book will astonish and amaze you and maybe even make you chuckle a little bit.

Before we get going there are a couple of technical notes pertaining to this book to mention. In the following pages you will find three types of font styles to help in clarifying who is saying what to whom.

This Arial italicized font that you are reading now depicts my narration of the story or necessary staging for the chat to come.

This Times New Roman bold font is my words when speaking and having a conversation with the animal or nature being.

This Times New Roman normal font is used when the animal or nature being is speaking.

The next bit of information that you need to know is that the words from animal or nature has not been edited at all. What is written down on paper during the time of the chat has not been changed or modified from its original wording, except for punctuation and spelling. If there is a need for further words to clarify the comment, these words are embraced in [brackets]. If there is additional information coming directly from the animal, it is embraced in (regular parenthesis).

These insights will certainly challenge your belief about what is possible from the minds of animal and nature. I know you will cherish these messages from animals and nature, as I have. And you may even learn a thing or two about yourself in the process. An offer is on the table to take a closer listen to the animals and nature beings that we have as neighbors and friends. Enjoy!

-Cynthia Attar

NOTE: If you are interested in communicating with animals and nature, I would like to recommend a great book, Profound Writings from Everyday People by Cynthia Attar. This book teaches that everyday people can learn to how to bring profound information down from upstairs, into their minds, and out their fingertips through writing (or typing). It also shows many others who are doing this work fluently and the book is ripe with every day people's submitted profound writings. Communicating with animals and nature uses this same technique and mental space. The only difference is that you learn to focus your mind on a specific animal/nature aspect, imagining you are right there inside the body of the being and then allow the thoughts to flow through freely.

Shetland at a Kiddy Pony Ride On:
Pride On A Job Well Done

When you live in rainy Portland Oregon and a sunny, dry Saturday in May presents itself, it warms your soul and fills it with gratitude. In the wake of long months of overcast and rainy winter days, a bright, sunny, dry morning is most appreciated by us Pacific Northwesters.

This day was one of those glory days, as I drove into our friend's driveway. Preschool aged children were riding tricycles in happy play. Through the mud-dotted windshield of Greenie, I caught a glimpse of the sight I really came to the party to see—kiddy Shetland pony rides in the backyard!

Four of the household family members had birthdays within 30 days of each other. Smartly and intuitively, the young mom decided to hold one big celebration to lump all birthdays into one special holiday. Today's highlight was for these city-raised youngsters to ride a real live pony!

Previously, I was aware of the limited four-hour early morning window of time that the ponies would be at the party providing child-thrilling adventures. Savoring this Saturday morning's opportunity to sleep in, absorb the newspaper, and linger for homemade brunch, my slow-moving husband and his brother couldn't fathom an urgency to start this day in a rush. In their opinion, the ponies could wait; but I couldn't! *Leaving those two lazy bones at home, I was anxious to arrive at the party during this narrow window of pony ride time.*

Upon arriving, I climbed out of Greenie, my nostalgic 1972 Ford F100 pickup, which served me well for 21 transportation years. The birthday family warmly shared their hugs and greetings. All attendees were in great spirits. The sun was accomplishing its springtime magic. After joyful introductions concluded between the other party-goers and myself, I smoothly slithered away to the back yard and began watching the two Shetlands do their job.

"Hm... quiet, obedient, good natured", I thought to myself. As a horse trainer it's impossible not to analyze animals and their handlers as to how they respond to each other. One pony mare was quiet, patiently waiting for a rider and was idle for a moment. The handler, a young man seemingly bored with his job, had a loose rein on the pony. I walked up to the handler and asked if I could talk to the calm mare. "Sure", the young teen replied, expecting me to do the normal nose petting, forelock stroking, and baby talk, like most people.

Approaching the small equine, I squatted down to her eye level. In introducing myself to her in a horse-horse way, I blew lightly into her nostrils. This not only told the horse who I was but opened the doors of communication between her and I. Taking a deep breath, I quieted my mind and tuned inwards. Immediately the pony ride pony said with tremendous pride:

"I give rides to children, and I am very good at it."

Now, I certainly did not make a living as an animal psychic. In fact, I had never even charged a dime to listen to any animals. I've tapped into their thoughts because I can and they seem to wish to express themselves. These in-service-to-human pets have profound insights if only we would–or could– hear them.

Normal animal psychics–if such a thing can be considered normal–usually do business with pet owners who have an inkling to believe in this level of telepathic, psychic communication. These owners have purposely called for the abnormal reading and have agreed to relinquish their hard-earned money for this service—generally to get specific questions answered from their beloved pet friend.

What I do is a bit different. I listen to the animals who spontaneously present themselves simply to be heard. In that, I subsequently have tossed myself in with pet owners and handlers whom, most likely, are a disbeliever of this type of nonverbal telepathic exchange of information. In these non-believing circles, I'm used to being thought of as weird, or—in the extreme—a nut case who should be thrown in the loony bin. I have taken much criticism when I talk/listen to animals, but it's not totally relevant what other people think of me. However, the sad thing is, this belief that animals cannot speak to humans leads people to disregard the valuable message coming from their own pet. I have willingly taken on the job of translating what the animals have to share and relay that back to the owner/handler—even if the person doesn't seem to want to hear or accept the message.

Most times I don't know how the animal's message will affect the owner. Maybe the owner needs the animal's message to solve a problem. Maybe the pet's message is exactly what the owner needs to hear for personal reasons, even if it doesn't seem so important to me. I purposely don't judge the message, I just relay it. And I feel a tremendous drive to do my translator job and get the information to the owners. Besides, I get real excited in telling people what the animals say. It's like listening to someone on the phone who has exciting news. It's imperative to relay that information to the rest of the household when you hang up. Especially since other people cannot hear on this phone!

I do know that everything a person hears is taken in and stored, even if not consciously processed or readily understood. This "seed message" wedges its way into a tiny corner of the vast subconscious mind and has the ability to be retrieved at some later date, if so chosen. All I can ask is that the message from the pet goes into the person's mind on some level. The person can do whatever s/he wants with it after that.

So in today's situation, I didn't know the handler–a teenage young man who probably had just taken an easy seasonal job. I didn't figure there was much value in even telling him how proud this mare was for doing such a good job. Nevertheless, in accordance with the moral commitment I had taken on, it was imperative to relay the seed message to the handler.

"She says she give rides to children, and is very good at it", I muttered to the young man on the opposite end of the loose lead rope. I never looked up at him nor spoke directly to his face. I just relayed the message for him to accept, ignore, or think I'm crazy. This particular handler seemed to simply ignore the message, as he was unresponsive.

I humbly thanked the pony for sharing her importance with me and walked away. As soon as I physically distanced myself from this working equine, I felt the powerful impact of her pride. Inside my body I felt a tremendous

8

rush of honor, value, and total worthiness. I felt humbled to nearly ego-less. I felt a high abundance of love for self and others.

This four legged pony angel was so proud to have a job in service to children, to be good at it, and to be loved for it. It seemed I was able to feel everything she was exuding. The emotional impact of this horse caused tears to well up inside me. I purposely tuned out all the party-goers hoping nobody would notice my highly emotional state of being. I reached in my bag and pulled out a pair of sunglasses to hide my teary eyes.

I really wanted to share the emotions of this pony mare with someone, as it affected me so deeply. I knew I was in a non-believing crowd so I wasn't sure how to accomplish this—or even if I would be able to. There were two women attending the birthday party that day who were open enough to consider that maybe I actually did hear the thoughts and feel the feelings of a pony-ride pony. Each woman in her own time came over to me noticing I was distancing myself from the human group. I told them both, but separately, what the little horse had said to me and the amount of pride she had for her seasonal job. Both women were cordial, polite, and non-offensive. One even found a tissue for me to wipe away the tears of emotion. Neither asked any questions about this conversation, was excited about this message, nor probably even believed it happened.

Deflated, I felt so alone in the middle of this large group of people. I had just shared a deep, loving bond with the Shetland pony and felt honored to be a part of it. Yet, I was unable to share it with any other human being. At that moment I was closer to this mare than any of the people around me.

This connection with animals, and the fact they trust me enough to share their innermost feelings, has changed me. My respect for all animals has increased drastically. It's disheartening to be bombarded by mainstream humans not willing to even consider that this type of nonverbal communication can occur.

As I see it, the bottom line is that I can pretend to be mainstream and do the typical unconscious playing, drinking, carousing, partying that most adults partake in. I can deny I heard the pony mare's heartfelt message. I can ignore the intense feelings of pride shared by a Shetland in a job well done. I can conform to get along with humans in their world of limited beliefs. However, my heart, my soul, and my deep desire is with the profound conversations I have with pets, animals, and other forms of nature. Today I present these conversations to honor my fellow beings; and to fulfill my "spokesperson" job to the best of my ability.

CHATS WITH PETS AND FARM ANIMALS

In this book, I have categorized pets as those animals, large and small, who live their life around humans. Since pets are so close to us, it seems that they experience our lives with us, which may distort their instinctual ways. The following chats with pets and farm animals reflect their words of profound insight of how life is for them.

Flo, the Suffolk Lamb, On:
Being Labeled a Dumb Animal

During my stay in LaCenter Washington, I took on a roommate to help pay the rent on a home which had about a quarter acre of yard. Mowing the lawn has always been my least favorite outdoor chore. In fact, I resisted this activity so dramatically that I refused to even own a lawn mower. Butch, my roommate, traveled with his work and couldn't commit to weekly mowings. Butch and I discussed the lawn mowing problem. If neither wanted to mow the lawn, who would? Would we hire out the dreaded job? Hm...maybe there was a better way to get the lawn mowed. We rationalized that instead of exerting money, energies, time, and frustration on personal upkeep of this huge lawn, we would acquire a couple "natural" lawn mowers who worked with little pay, and also had built in fertilizing capabilities—lambs.

One day Butch brought home two of the most darling Suffolk lambs. The names they gave me were Moe and Flo, male and female, respectively. This was my first experience with raising lambs. They were of great joy to have around. Their bleating was idyllic for the farm life in amongst the other coexistent creatures. Yet, these addictive animals were somewhat irritating, as they seemed to be obsessed with food.

Being sort of shy at first, once these lambs realized that the yummy morning grain came from me, both Moe and Flo were my best friends. The most fun time I had with my lawn mowers was when I would sit in their field (the front yard) with some grain and they would climb nearly on top of me to eat it out of my hands. When the grain was gone, these funny critters would entertain themselves by exploring this strange human and courageously sticking their nose in my hair or face. Of course I had to give them a voice. Flo seemed to be the leader and the one most interested in chatting with me in a direct manner. I was in for a huge surprise with this outspoken, wise ewe.

Hi lambs. Here I am to chat. How's life for you two?

Do you have food?

No.

Why not?

Because you seem too dependent on oats.

What are you doing?

Just sitting and talking to you.

You think we are dumb?

I guess I do. That's what people say. Are you?

Heavens, you just don't know us and how we think. Dumb in is the mind of the beholder.

So, tell me more.

You [humans] see dumb. We represent the 'dumb' parts of humans, those who follow and not lead. Those who don't think for themselves. That, to you, is dumb. We [sheep] survive. We have survived for centuries. You think a dumb animal would do that? We think collectively. We all have thoughts, but they are conjoined, or meshed with our brothers and sisters. And it all comes as one thought. We then act on the one thought. What would happen if we did otherwise? We wouldn't be sheep. We would be cows or some other creature. We are the unity that humans are afraid of. We are conjoined, we think collectively, we act collectively. We are one. How many humans do this?

No, what I see is that humans WANT to do this, but then they don't. They hate us for not thinking for ourselves, call us dumb, devalue us, etc. There seems to be a dual pull in humans—to be conjoined and to be separate. This creates confusion, destruction, hatred, and many bad attributes. We have no such dual pull. We are one, and display that proudly as that is our basic essence. Humans judge us for this as they have a belief that separate is better.

How many trees have we cut? How many forests have we destroyed? How much earth destruction have we participated in? Not much, if any. Can't say that for separate, judgmental humans who want to think they are superior to us 'dumb' sheep. We nourish the earth, we provide for growth, not destroy. You hate us as you hate that inherent part of yourself that is dependent and collective. And it IS inherent. We all are one. You humans just deny yours, we don't. We stare you in the face and say, "Look at yourself. You are just like us. If you hate us, then you hate this aspect of yourself. If you love us, then you love that aspect of yourself. We are all one, whether you all *think* you are separate or not." Thank you for giving us a voice. If a 'dumb' sheep can help with the title of this book, try <u>Giving a Voice to those Dumb, Crippled, Inferior Slobs that are…..ME</u>

I don't know about that. I may have to modify it a bit, but I hear you and will take it into consideration. Thank you.

Whenever you want another 'dumb' conversation, you are welcome to it.

Thank you. I value you much more and see your insightful wisdom.

You are welcome.

August, the Persian Cat, On:
The Benefits of Purring

Years prior it became apparent that if I was to further my self-worth I must quit frequenting cocktail lounges and the drinking of alcohol—which had been my means of social interaction. Living alone and sober, it quickly became more difficult to connect with people, so I sought out alternative ways to fulfill my ailing social life. Substituting for the liquor bars, I began hanging out at coffee counter cafés, who employed personable wait staff, and preferably drew in talkative customers.

On this particular day, I was sitting at such a counter in a local truck stop hangout near my home. As usual, I was chatting with the waitress about various subjects. I casually mentioned my desire to acquire a cat to temper the rampant mouse population around the house. This waitress mentioned she was frustrated with her two cats at home that fought quite frequently. She then quickly disappeared into the kitchen to retrieve a hot and ready meal.

About twenty minutes later during this disjointed on/off discussion about the state of cats in her house and other issues, her husband "coincidentally" arrived at the restaurant with a beautiful, long haired, white with blue points, pug faced kitty. It just happened to be the difficult feline in the waitress's household. Apparently, on one of her trips to the kitchen, the waitress sneaked in a phone call to her husband to bring the unwanted cat to her workplace—'just in case' I was interested in taking her home to help control the rising mouse population. How could I say no to this high expectation offer? Besides, this fuzzy feline ball was in my heart immediately.

That day I left home for a cup of coffee and a bit of human interaction, and returned with a kitty companion! August, the Persian-Himalayan cat, stayed with me during the best and worst of times for the next nine years. This amazing cat tolerated many homes, many environments, and was my consistent friend. With every household move I insisted on a good home for August where she could be inside or outside at her own desire.

One day I was feeling particularly frustrated by unsolicited negative opinions of these telepathic animal chats. August decided she had something to say about it.

August, do you have something to say for a cat chat?

Don't let those people upset you–those that ridicule what you are doing. Your chats are a service to all humans and all animals, even if some humans do not recognize it. We value what you are doing and that you are trying to get the word out that we have a voice and we do want to be heard. And we are here for you (speaking collectively), so you can evolve. When you evolve, we can evolve and be more peaceful. And isn't that what we all want is inner peace and to purr?

If humans could only purr it would give them a measure of when they were in peace. Sometimes humans are in peace more often than they realize, yet their lack of purring makes them think they are not. If they would purr it would make them aware of their peaceful times and then they can build on that peace and purr more. It would be a verbal display of what is going on inside. The reason cat purrs calm people is because it is as though we say we accept you and want to be with you—that you are okay, which is all that humans want to know—that they are okay. And if they are okay around a cat at that precise moment, it brings a calmness in their being. As you know, all illnesses are created by a lack of purring. And when we go into elder homes [residences for senior living centers] and we purr, we balance them for those moments we purr and make them okay again, if only for a moment, until we get scared or move away. We do a grand service to people in our purring, as there is no better state of mind than inner peace.

Well said. Thank you, August.

Cats On: Being a Solitary Animal

It's a lonely life we live. We want to be with others but cannot. We represent the cat. Inherently alone, we do enjoy company of other animals and humans. Our natural instinctual lifestyle has been taken away. No longer do we hunt for our food or build our homes. Food and home is provided now so our energy is low. As a solitary animal, that means we do not want to compete with another for food and attention. If we have been alone, we prefer that. (Kittens love to be with other kittens, cats want to be alone). If another animal in the household accepts us as number one we are fine with them and enjoy their company, especially when our person is gone.

Thank you, August.

Cats On: Life Can Be Fun!

Later, I had two cats that stuck around for many years. They were great mousers for the farm and loved to rule over the dogs. Della and Tickle both wanted to contribute to a cat chat.

We love the life of the farm cat. We love the freedom, the air, the play of the mouse. It is our desire to live our lives out here in the mystery of this farm. There are birds to stalk, mouse to play with, warm beds to sleep in, and food in abundance. We even love to play with the other animals and enjoy the excitement of being chased. We know we will always win the chase, so it is non-threatening. We love to be squirrelly and run from danger, even if there is no danger. Life doesn't have to be stressful. It can be fun.

White Pheasant On:
Angels Come in Many Forms

After being my companion for nearly nine years, August, my precious and highly tolerant cat, disappeared into the dark of the night. There didn't seem to be any specific reason for her leaving. All was well in the household, and life was actually fairly quiet at the time. August was not ailing in physical health or displayed any unusual behaviors. I wasn't able to comprehend why she left. She had been my faithful companion for so long, under difficult circumstances and joyful times. About a week after August left, a strange phenomenon happened.

I drove into the driveway at home one afternoon and my roommate, Butch, met me at the car. He was visibly confused and began to rattle on about this strangely colored pheasant that had earlier been wandering about the yard. Apparently this critter had the typical pheasant coloring on his body, but he carried on his back, two totally white wings. Butch was a reasonable, logical guy who had not partook in any chemical substance for the last eight years. I knew Butch wasn't making this up, but sort of wrote it off as probably an incident exclusive for Butch for some unknown reason that only he could someday unravel.

I went on with life and two or three days later when Butch was not home, outside the kitchen window I noticed an unusual large bird. Quietly I snuck outside for a closer look at this beautiful creature, trying not to scare him away. Sure enough, this fowl was exactly what Butch had described! What a treat to see a white pheasant on my property. I had never seen such a gorgeous pheasant with solid white wings. I concluded that this unusually

18

colored bird may not have been an exclusive message for Butch, but could have possibly been for me, too. Watching until the bird walked away and around the corner, I felt compelled to have a conversation with this white pheasant. I ran into the house and picked up my chat notebook.

I'd like to talk to the white pheasant, please. Pheasant, I think you came here for a reason—to give us a message or something. I haven't got your message, so can you be clear?

Remember when Sally was lost and Lydia said she was with a white mule?

Yes.

(Sally, my mule, literally got away from me on a camping trip and subsequently got herself lost in the woods. I searched for her for, days and into weeks. What finally lead me to Sally's whereabouts was a session with a fabulous animal communicator, Lydia Hiby. Lydia received vital information, direct from Sally herself, to assist the search and rescue of my valued mule. Lydia told me that Sally had run into a white mule who became her buddy and helped her to stay safe until we finally found and rescued her.)

And there was no such white mule?

Yes.

Was Lydia wrong?

I don't know. Maybe Sally *was* with a white mule, sort of holographically or imaginary, or an angel that which was perceived by Sally, but not by anyone else.

Keep going. Who was I to you?

White, a sign of angels. You were a pheasant who definitely wanted our attention for some reason that I am unaware. Who are you?

I am a messenger. You got that right.

What is the message you are bringing? I'd like to know, but fear I can't get it or will hear wrong.

Would time help to get it right?

No. Confidence would help.

Well, here is one dose of confidence. (Whispers) Listen closely. What do you hear?

My crying inside. My crying inside.

What else?

August.

What is she saying?

August (my cat that left) came through easily.

AUGUST: I am okay. You didn't make me leave. I just left.

Why, after all this time? We had nine years together. Why did you go?

AUGUST: I had to—it was time.

No other explanation?

AUGUST: I was drawn. I don't know why. I never question my draws, I just act on them.

Ok, were you drawn away from home and me, or towards something else?

AUGUST: Towards another home, another situation, another life.

How could you leave me?

AUGUST: I wasn't needed, just wanted.

But you *were* wanted.

AUGUST: Yes, but I had lived out that part of my life. Now it's time I worked again. I am drawn to an active life—one where my services are again needed. I like being a helper cat. Cheyenne left to be a helper dog.

(Cheyenne was a German Shepherd dog who was with me twice. Chats with Cheyenne are in later chapters.)

I guess I am not-needy?

AUGUST: Isn't that why you are alone?

Could be, I don't NEED anyone. So, August, who is White Pheasant?

AUGUST: An attention-getter. I sent him as his coloring and uniqueness would get your attention.

And why did you want my attention?

AUGUST: To relay that I was okay.

And?

AUGUST: Well, I know you wanted to know why I left.   And began to blame yourself.

The chat continued, as I asked August some personal questions which I have omitted from this text. It is my opinion that the white pheasant came to me as—or representing—August, to deliver a message. When his job was done, the white pheasant retreated back to source. I've since researched through internet, yet have been unable to identify such a white winged pheasant type bird. Maybe, just as Sally's angel white mule who assisted her when she was lost, this angel pheasant with snow white wings assisted me in my confusion when August disappeared.

Fred, the Banty Rooster, On:
Dog Attack & Surviving

Having free roaming chickens was great happiness for both me and these farm poultry. They were very content to have a home, food, and water provided, yet free to wander wherever they wanted. At the time of this chat, I had yet to build a proper chicken coop or secure the yard with chicken wire. It was on my to-do list, but a horse fence was my first priority on this newly purchased farm property. The only problem the chickens encountered from this situation was one day the neighbor dog decided to "play" with Fred, the Banty rooster. This dog decided to chase, catch, and then carry home my beloved rooster in his jaws. Luckily, the dog owners were privy to the incident in time to save the life of Fred the rooster. Once retrieved and brought back to our farm, Fred was very shaken up and extremely dependent on me to help him in his time of need. He withdrew and hid in a dark corner, scared to death to come out.

Fred, I'd like a conversation with you if you don't mind.

Don't want to talk now. Too frightened.

I should have respected Fred's wishes, but for some reason I felt the urge to push onwards.

How can I help you, Fred?

You can put Betty (his hen pal) with me, this would help me. I think I am safe, but not sure. Dark corner feels safer.

What was the purpose of the incident?

I hate to be part of your learnings, but I had to go through it for you. I mean, I hate to be nearly dead for you to learn. That part of death that is right before death, is not easy.

The suffering?

The knowing you are going to die. Or thinking you may die. We don't want that any more than humans. We fight for our lives too. It's nature's way. Fear makes us fight for our lives. That is the hard part. The death is easy, the fight to stay alive is hard.

How are you doing tonight?

Cold, sore, crying inside.

I'm so sorry. I will get you both [Fred and Betty] a much better home soon.

Just want to sleep. Hurt.

Tell me why you did this for me.

Your victimization problem. How I was victimized, is you. You handled it very well, I do say. You took that which was in front of you (the rooster/dog crisis) and didn't blame. You took the incident and moved on, upwards. You did not become victim to the neighbor's dog, the neighbors, or the incident. You did not decide you had to bail out, or change homes, or run away. You dealt with it as a grown up person should, as we chickens do. We just move on from this moment, every moment. We accept all for right now, as of now. Think that….as of now. You passed the test.

Tell me something else, Fred.

Chickens. Chickens are things people eat. They think nothing about it when opening a food store package or see some scraggly animated chicken on TV [ads]. Chickens are not highly valued with humans, but chickens can be a tremendous and valuable teacher.

How?

First, you know chickens are one who are afraid and run [or fly].

Yes, high flight instinct.

You even have a word for humans who are afraid to fight and [would rather] run away… "chicken."

Yes, we do. It's not a pleasant word, sort of degrading. I don't like that, but I see it now much clearer.

So, as chickens, we are nothing to humans. No, not nothing, we are less than nothing. We are things to poop on. We are laughed at, ridiculed, unvalued and such, by humans. BUT, look at who is saying those words, thinking those thoughts? Those who feel this inside themselves. Be honored you love chickens, because that means you love yourself. When you can see value and importance to even those smallest of creatures, and especially to the creatures that the rest of society degrades, you are a valuable person in yourself. My incident today was to get you to talk to me and let me show you a vulnerable side of you. The chicken side of you. The side that wants to run away at signs of danger coming near. As you know, running does not get you anywhere, as it never gets chickens anywhere but dead. As you run, those you are running from, chase. And it gets more intense and more intense until something happens that you don't want. Either you are overcome by the chaser or you get to hide for a little bit until the dog [the problem] goes away for now. But you know the dog [problem] will come back, as the dog [problem] lives next door. Point is, running will not get you away from that which you are running from, as that which you are running from lives next door and will again find you.

What is the best thing to do instead of run?

You see how you like prey animals on the farm. This is representative in you. You feel like prey sometimes and that other humans are the predators.

Ok, I see that now. I am most attracted to prey animals rather than predatory animals. What do I do about this bit of information?

Study why you don't like predators. What is it in them that repulses you? Why do you choose to be chicken and run? Why do you enjoy gentling those afraid? Why not work with predators? Think about this for a minute and you will find that predators are what *you* are. This needs to be toned down and balance is the key. This is what is stopping you from being one with animals. There is a predator/prey attitude here and we are here to help you balance that out. Think about this and if there is more information you need,

I will be here for you. In the meantime I need sleep and warmth and to dispel my fears. Thank you. Night.

Thank you SO much Fred.

I was able to get Betty in with him that night and then bought a heat lamp the next day to keep him a bit warmer. His fear and attitude was depressed for about a week. Eventually, he came out of the near death incident just fine. About a year later, Fred succumbed to a hungry, stray dog.

Rita, the Guinea Pig, On:
Silent Royalty

At one time a lady contacted me about giving her precious guinea pig a reading. She was very proud of her guinea and wanted to show him and the species off to anyone who would listen. This lady presented me with a picture of a very cute little animal. I had never had a chat with a guinea pig, so I was curious as to what profound insights were to come from Rita, the guinea pig.

Rita, do you want to talk to me? Please present yourself.

I am here. I will represent guinea pigs of all guinea pigs. We have such a treat to show with humans. And only the select few who value our potential will benefit from us. We are elegant and highly worthwhile. It is our purpose to help humans to get back to their instinctual nature. In that, I mean one must feel the right things, do the right things, and be the right person.

We guinea pigs are not from the wild like most animals that you are aware of. Not in this country, in this form. We are bred and stay alive for humans. Therefore we give our love to them. But they have to earn our love. We do not give freely like a dog, we only give freely to those who value and appreciate us. We, for the most part, stay silent. And when we find a human who values us, then our personality shines and we affect that one person profoundly. The relationship between guinea pig and human rarely goes beyond that one human. An individual relationship, but the human is changed forever when s/he enters a relationship with a guinea pig. We are grand animals and value life and play. Anyone who has had a close relationship with a guinea pig will tell you the immense benefits. We are not here to spout off how wonderful we are. When you enter into a guinea pig /human relationship, that will become very apparent.

Thank you for your insight, Rita.

Willie, the Australian Shepherd, On:
Adjusting to a New Home

Willie came to my home via a roommate situation. His person, Butch, was working temporarily in the area and needed a place to hang his hat where he could have his Australian Shepherd dog with him. Willie went nearly everywhere with Butch, and was a perfect gentlemen at home with my animals—even the three free roaming chickens. I snatched an opportunity to see how Willie felt about our little farm and the critters around the place.

How do you like it here, Willie?

I like it when Dad is with me and I with him. I like anything. He is my home. Where he is, is my home. I can adjust to many areas of the country, many other animals, many other circumstances and people. As long as I am with him and he with me. I love the space here [at the farm]. I love the roominess. I love the variety of animals. I'm sort of afraid when they chase me, though. (Speaking about Satchmo, the donkey, and his dog chasing habit—which we will get into later). I don't know why they do that. I am learning to be aware and stay out of their way. I learned to do that before. I know those ropes. (Willie was trained as a working cattle dog). I just haven't had to be in that situation recently. I remember.

What about your old place and friends and people and all. Do you miss them?

All is well with me. It is my Dad that is my concern. As happy as he is, that is how I am. He is more relaxed here. Sort of antsy, but liking it.

What are your worries or concerns?

I want to be with Dad. I don't like to be separated, put outside. Seems some women come into his life and I am shut out more than when one isn't in his life. I don't resent the person, just have to remind him that I am here and that I still want to be with him.

I understand. Anything else?

I love the treats. There are more in there (Willie was speaking about a low to the ground cupboard that houses a stash of doggy treats), I can smell them. This will be a fun place to explore. Food in many corners, many cupboards. The home is spacious and doggy. There was a dog in here before, so it's not sterile like some places. I feel at home here.

What about the cat? (August)

Well, it's her home. I will share. She sets the rules and that's fine with me.

How can I make your stay good?

Just pet me when I ask, keep me with Dad, and give me treats. You are a kind person and care about me. I like you, too. I think you have a brush. Will you brush me, too? Like you do with the cat?

Oh, August has told you that, huh?

Yes, the cat has told me many things so far.

Like what?

Like she has the blue chair (my personal leather recliner I've hauled with me through many moves). Like, she has your lap. Like, she has your room. She is okay with me on my side of the house and she will share the common rooms. We know our places. She rules. She says you feed her and pet her and love her and brush her and are real good to her. That makes me like you too.

Anything about Dad you want him to know?

His feet. I keep trying to help his feet, but I can't seem to fix them. I don't know what to do to fix his feet. I will help heal all I can. Your feet, too. (Willie had this insatiable urge to lick my feet. It was later revealed that he does this with Butch, too).

Anything else?

You bring out a gentler side of him than some people. I like that gentler side. The harder [more stressed] he is, the roughness comes out of him. It's fine, but he's not as attentive to me.

Thank you very much, Willie.

Dicky Doo, the Xolo Dog, On:
A Walk-in to a Cat Body

Living outside of Yakima Washington in the remote desert, there were wild predators to be concerned about regarding the safety of my small array of animals. Usually the concern was focused around the coyotes, with a few other critters in the mix. The elk and deer that grazed across the highway each evening were a blessing, not a threat. However, the most unfeeling predator was certainly the semi-trucks and vehicles blazing quickly past on the highway in front of my land. It was an ongoing task to make sure the dogs and cats stuck around inside the fence line. In the event a deer was hit by a car, this task became especially vigilant, as Dicky Doo, one of my Xoloitzcuintle dogs (shortened to Xolo, [pronounced, "sho-lo"]), became determined to escape the fenced yard to drag home a deer leg. One Saturday morning Dicky Doo finally succumbed to the most dangerous predator in the area, the 18 wheeler semi-truck. After I scraped his scattered, bloody body parts from the highway, I had to have a conversation with Dicky to make sure he was okay in his transition.

Dicky Doo, tell me what is going on with you now. Are you okay?

A part of me is observing the death of my physical body. And remembering the life I lived. I'm glad I could be "part of the wild" in death. That was the most exciting part of living remotely—wild all around, and to really be a part of it is an honor. I really enjoyed my time on the farm. I knew there were risks. And that was what was so much fun. But I could go only as far as I did. Tai Chi (the other Xolo dog, and his buddy) is a better dog for you, in that she is more content to just be with you than I was. I loved being with you, but wanted more time with you. I also wanted adventure more than she. She is a good dog for you and will serve you well for years. About me, I'll still be in the wild, but a bit more reserve—as the new black cat. (I had just a couple days prior obtained a feral black cat to help temper the growing mice population.) It's my way of getting that wild freedom without harming you.

Are you now adjusting to being in a cat body?

Give me a few days. The cat knows how to be in a cat body, but my mind isn't quite there yet. It's not like I won't be able to walk, jump, climb right away. The cat part knows that. I'm just taking the mind of the cat. And it may take a day or so to adjust. Don't be surprised if you find me on your lap one winter evening in the chair. It will be me, Dicky Doo.

Okay, I will remember.

Dicky Doo On:
People Abusing Animals

Dogs love their people. Even if the people are not capable of loving them. People are of all different stages. Some can love dogs deeply and some tie them up and don't think of them as souls. All ranges on the spectrum are okay. We all are here to benefit ourselves and the lives of our people. Take just one person who gets a dog and tethers him for all his life, like Dick (the guy who intended to kill Dicky Doo before I rescued him). That person cannot see or feel the love we dogs naturally possess. But it still is there. Maybe one day that person will be able to feel love. And when they do, they will remember us and that radiation of love we all have. We will have been of use to that person in their development.

But what about the life of an abused dog like that?

We still are trying to reach people and believe it or not, we are part of their process of change and growth. As a person grows, they learn new and different things. What you see when someone is abusing an animal, in a while, they may not do that anymore because they know more now. They have grown and learned and changed. The abused dog was part of their learning. Again, as you have heard before, we are helping you people to evolve in whatever way we can. If that means taking abuse, so be it. We don't see it as abuse like people do. We see it as having a stronger impact on a person's life that needed it to become better, more at peace. Occasionally we will draw weary of the abuse and end our life, but mostly we are there to help the advancement of people. Sometimes a dog comes into the life of a person who has health issues. And that dog helps the health issues. Maybe by taking attention off of the person by having their own health issues, or maybe by healing in a dog-love way. Whatever way we can help people to become more loving and at peace, that is our goal. We are not relegated to one way of being, we can reach more in different ways. Today is one of adjustment. I will be seeing you soon. Remember, the black cat is me.

Okay, Dicky. I am so sorry that you have left me as a dog. You did great. You are a gem. From when you came to me with no discipline, out of control, I didn't think I'd ever get you trained. But you came around and were a GREAT dog, perfect for me. You taught Tai Chi about being a dog, about being with people, about being on the farm. You did a fabulous job in tracking, agility, and getting along with the other animals, too. I will miss you as a dog in my life. So will Tai Chi. Best to you and I'll be watching for you to come around, my new black cat.

Cheyenne, the German Shepherd, On:
The Importance of Smelling & Barking

A while back I acquired a beautiful female German Shepherd dog. Not having a dog for several years, Cheyenne was a welcome part of my family— well, August, the cat, may not have agreed with that! Cheyenne seemed to be nearly obsessive with having to smell every single thing. So I asked her about it. Her answers reminded me to be in the moment.

Cheyenne, why do you smell everything?

There are so many smells in the air when the wind blows. Point upwind and just sniff. That will tell me which direction to travel. I travel towards the best smell. Sometimes I get off the track of that smell onto another interesting smell.

What happens when you reach that smell source?

Then I check it out and see if I want to eat it, roll in it, or play with it.

Our house is a short walk to the river. Between the house and the river is undeveloped land where many locals go for walks. Another trait of Cheyenne is that she barks at folks walking way down by the river, but if someone comes to the door, she won't make a sound. For better understanding, I asked her about this.

Why do you bark at things way off in the distance?

Sometimes I see/smell/sense something I'm not sure what it is. I bark to identify myself. "I am a dog, what are you?" Sometimes a noise/bark is in reply. Then I can better determine if it's friend or foe. When there is no reply, I keep asking. Barking protects me. I feel surrounded by my barks as a shield against whatever I sense out there.

Do you have anything else you want to say?

I like the game you taught me today [retrieve]. That is something that you and I can do together that I think YOU will like. Please do more of that. Any interaction you have with me is welcome. The more interaction, the more obedient I become. The less interaction, the less obedient I am, as I have to take it upon myself to entertain myself and that may not be in a way you approve of. I just want to be with you and have you and I interact. When you are not around, I do what I can to keep you there with me—such as pull clothes [out of laundry basket or off the clothesline] that have your smell on them, [and take them] out where I am. Makes me feel like you are nearby.

Thank you Cheyenne.

Shatki, the German Shepherd, On:
Dog Reincarnation

Before I acquired Cheyenne, I had a very similar dog named Shatki. Shatki was my companion during homeless times when Greenie, the 72 Ford pickup, was our only home. One of our adventures during that era was taking on a volunteer job as a summer campground host at a horse camp in the Mt. St. Helens National Recreation Area. Even with my love of nature, I hadn't been too much into taking camping trips. It made more sense to live in the woods than visit occasionally, so that's what I decided to do.

I hauled Sally the mule, Zip the horse, August the cat, & Shatki the dog, up into the wilderness for our summer job. We were offered a little self-contained camp trailer owned by the U.S. Forest Service. My animal family and I spent a few months as close to heaven as it could possibly get! This was an extremely beneficial time for my peace of mind. It was at the horse camp where I realized the deep seated desire to own my own secluded, nature-surrounding farm.

It was in our little slice of heaven where Shatki decided to leave one night, similar to August's unexpected disappearance in a former story. Late one evening, very nearby, the woodsy silence was disrupted by howling of coyotes. The next day, Cheyenne had disappeared—without a trace. My distant telepathic communications indicated that my valued angel friend had went running with these dogs and was in complete joy. Shatki said she had

36

come to help me through some tough times and now this job was done. It was time she moved on to the next phase in her life. I missed her terribly.

A few years later, my inner urging to get another dog surfaced. That is when I found Cheyenne. The first evening upon ownership of this new young German Shepherd dog, Cheyenne eagerly jumped into the middle of Greenie's bench seat and naturally settled in laying down with her head on my lap. I was overcome with the intense—but totally at home—feeling that I was with Shatki again. I wondered if the two were the same. One day I decided to try and connect with Shatki, through Cheyenne, and was able to do so. I asked Shatki about the Cheyenne connection.

SHATKI: It is I in another body. Sometimes she [Cheyenne] knows it, sometimes she doesn't. My time with you was short last time. I was called upon to assist you through. I am an angel. I have materialized in many forms to assist you along. I am here, now, as you will need stabilization in the near future. I will help to keep you focused on your goals, reminding you constantly to be in nature. I am your motivation to go where it is calling you.

As with Shatki, Cheyenne ran away abruptly after about three years with me and never returned. She said she was finished with our job together and wanted to play with kids for a while.

Neighborhood Dog On:
The Joy of Playing

One favorite activity when living in Lyle Washington was to take Cheyenne for a walk down to the Columbia River. On this particular day, I took my note pad to the river's edge and peacefully sat on a large rock.

"How about a chat? Anyone want to talk to me?"

There is a dog in the neighborhood. I thought it was the neighborhood dog whom I was talking to, but it could have been Cheyenne.

DOG: When you see me running and playing I do it for me exclusively. Joy radiates out from me, but I can only hope that you are affected by it. I do it for me. If humans could be fun and play, it would radiate out to other beings who would be affected by that, who would want to run and play.

Just then, Cheyenne shocked me by sticking her nose right smack in my face.

As animals wanting humans to evolve, all we want is for humans to love life in the moment as we do. We are only examples for you, in hopes that you will follow our example. Remember when you were a kid and you loved to play in the sand and get dirty? That's us. We love to get dirty 'cause it's all play, it's all fun, it's the moment. We don't worry about cleaning ourselves up at that moment. We "worry" about what we want right now. And how to express what's going on inside. Right now I have much energy 'cause I don't have to worry about anything now.

Spokesdog On:
The Inevitable Destruction of Earth;
And Five Minutes to Happiness

In talking to dogs, I quite often receive similar information—that basically dogs are our role models. And if we can model ourselves after them in unconditional love, joy, play, and being in the moment we would better our lives. And they are here to help us do just that. Recently, I wanted more in-depth words of wisdom, so I asked to speak with a dog who would act as a 'spokesdog' and enlighten me further on our path of awareness. I sensed an urgency of his message.

We can go on for hours and days and months and years telling you to use dogs as your example in living lives. Live for the moment, be loyal, love everything, but it seems as though it's not getting through. So, we need to talk to you humans in a different way.

Time is of the essence. This place [earth] is falling apart. Your attitudes are self-destructing your planet. It is no longer adequate for us to tell you to be like a dog. You are past the breaking point. More has to occur now for the proper change.

We dogs will "go" happy, you will go sad and unfulfilled. Make it every person's goal at this moment, that if you do self-destruct and the earth is gone, that you will go happy. So, every one of you, right now, today, has to make the decision on what it takes to be happy—and do it. Take five minutes and be happy. I ask of you today. Be happy for five minutes. Feel it. Express every happy emotion that you know.

If you don't know how to be happy, experiment. Try until you get good and you truly are happy for five minutes. And time it. Some guidelines for being happy: Look at the exact moment that you are at. Not the past moment or the future moment, but the exact moment and be in the moment for five minutes.

See what is in front of you and appreciate it. Learn the value of appreciation. Humans are the only animal who hold the gift of appreciation. Love and appreciation are two different things. Notice the difference. Forget your past, forget your future. At every moment, think, "What do I want to do?" Not "What should I do?", "What do I need to do?", "What are my responsibilities?", "What will I be glad I did later?" But, "What do I want to do right this minute?", "What will make me happy?" Think of that activity and how you will feel doing it. Not afterwards, but right at this moment. If it will make you feel happy doing it, let that be your guide for your five minutes of happiness. Take minutes out of every day, on a schedule if needed, to be happy. Just as you schedule your exercise or your eating, commit to five minutes of happiness every day. I ask this of you. Let today be day one for this exercise. It will be your salvation in times to come.

The Equine Story

Several years ago, the two equines in my ownership consisted of Sally, a molly mule, and Zip, an Appaloosa horse gelding. Sally came to me when she was just 2 years old as an untrained mule filly. Zip, I acquired years earlier at the ripe old age of 16. I was concerned how many years he actually had left in him, knowing a horse's life-span typically is between 20-25 years. Little did I know at the time, Zip would be with me for quite a spell.

I was at a crossroads in my life. One day I received a timely phone call from a notable, fairly wealthy businessman four hours north of where I was living. This gentleman had his own construction business but his love was to pack with horses and mules fairly steadily in the summertime. The purpose of the phone call was his request to lease my beloved Sally mule to be part of his pack mule string for a couple of summers. I thought this offer would be a good learning opportunity for her, as I was not able to provide her with a job. I agreed to his offer under one condition: the packer would have to take both Sally and Zip. For the lease of Sally to work on his pack string, the man would have to keep and feed both equines for two winters. Sally was just nine years old at this time and Zip was getting to be an old man at age 28. Not having responsibility for large equines for a while was attractive to me. This would give me the freedom of no large animals, the first time in 13 years. This arrangement would also free me up to move residences and experience the city life for the first time. The timing just happened to coincide with embarking on another new adventure—marriage to a city-raised man.

The packer agreed to my conditions and it wasn't long before both animals were shipped off to "summer (and winter) camp". Soon, Sally was packing in the high country, learning about life as a pack mule; and Zip was retired, mingling around with other mules and horses in the packer's field. During the second winter part of the lease, the businessman told me that Zip began losing weight and his will to live. The packer decided that it was the end of Zip's life and he was going to arrange the veterinarian to come out and put him out of his misery.

Extremely distraught, I felt I didn't have many choices where Zip was concerned. My husband and I were living near downtown Portland Oregon and were very tight financially. I had no place to keep Zip and no money to board him out. I didn't know what else to do except to trust this guy's judgment and figured Zip's time was probably up. Hey, I rationalized, the four legged guy was pushing 30 years old—way past his expected life-span. I took a few days off work and my husband and I drove north to say a last good-bye to my beloved Appaloosa friend. It was an extremely emotional scene and the new groom didn't really know what to do with his sobbing bride. After the final salutations, we somberly headed back home to Portland. I mourned terribly for the horse I cherished for 13 years. Slowly I adjusted to never seeing my beloved Zip again.

A short while later, the packer called about Sally, and mentioned Zip and how he was doing. You could have knocked me over with a feather! Last I was informed, Zip should have been dead! Apparently, that did not happen. I later learned that once the veterinarian showed up, the horse doctor refused to euthanize the old guy, stating that Zip only needed his teeth floated (filed down) to be able to eat and gain weight again. The packer forgot to tell me this valuable tidbit of information about Zip.

A similar situation happened again with this packer and Zip. And once again, Zip secretly lived on when I was told he was going to be—and expected him to be—expired. I wasn't happy with this situation and I finally was able to scrape together minimal finances. After extensive searching, I found a place to house the equines outside Portland. A horse friend offered to drive me, with her pickup and horse trailer, to get Zip and Sally. We began our trek—the four hour drive north to the expensive, upper class farm—to take Sally and Zip back to the Portland outskirts.

43

Once I found the particular pasture where they were located, I spotted Sally and called to her. Immediately her nose popped up out of the grass, as she recognized my voice. Sally came a-running at a gallop when she heard me call, but Zip was nowhere to be found. Truly questioning the sanity of this wealthy businessman, I wasn't sure if Zip was currently alive or dead. I knew I had to at least rescue Sally from this living arrangement. My beloved mule loaded into the trailer gracefully, willingly, and we headed south towards Portland.

It took a few months of detective work to figure out where Zip was residing. The story goes that the vet thrice again was called out to end Zip's life. The doctor again questioned the packer on his decision to exterminate a horse that just needed a bit more maintenance. This local prestigious businessman said that Zip's skinny body made him look like he wasn't taking care of Zip and other people would question if he was taking care of his other animals. Apparently, having a weak looking old horse in his field threatened his golden boy reputation. Nevertheless, the vet was unable to kill a horse just because of inconvenience and [seeming] reputation of some wealthy jock. Not knowing that Zip did not belong to the packer, I had learned that this doctor offered to take Zip off this man's hands by placing Zip on his (the vet) sister's farm with Candy, an older Arabian mare, in a nearby town.

Attempting to track down which vet was coming out to euthanize Zip; through the process of elimination, I eventually landed upon the particular office which this packer-man was a client. Luckily, I was able to convince the animal doctor that I was Zip's actual owner and soon I had a link to Zip's whereabouts. Another trip up north was in play as I scanned my Thomas Guide map to locate the address of the veterinarian's sister's farm.

The location turned out to house huge barns, in an upper class farming neighborhood, surrounded by numerous dairies. Wow, what a place to call home. At the particular address, I knocked on the front door, but the owners were not home. I took the liberty to scout around this beautiful homestead. Ah yes, way in the back in a little field I spotted my honored Zip and a mare.

Zip wasn't as alert as I remembered, but he seemed to know who I was. Upon close examination, Zip looked horrible. He had the runs and his rear end was caked with manure. He hadn't seen a brush for months, and his eyes were filled with sleep. I found a brush and cleaned him up as best I could. It was winter, so I was unable to give him a proper bath and cleansing. I noticed Zip had hay in the manger and he seemed to get along well with his girlfriend, Candy, an aged Arabian mare. I didn't have too many options, so I left a note on the residence's door with my contact information.

Back to Portland I headed, stressed out and confused as to what to do. Soon, Candy's owner called me and we talked. Knowing more about cows, these folks were only minimally horse educated. I offered to supply anything I could to assist them in adequate care for Zip. The wife was very polite, and I could tell they just didn't know much about proper horse care. I sent some grooming items complete with helpful notes on the care of horses. I wasn't in a financial position to take Zip back, and really didn't want to separate him from his girlfriend.

On subsequent trips up north, I found Zip to be in adequate shape, sometimes even happy and content. My assumption was that Zip and Candy would stay at Candy's home for the duration of their aging lives. It wasn't a perfect home, but it was better than the last place with the packer man.

In the meantime, the boarding home that I found for Sally was one which was peppered with many equines. During that time, my typically infertile mule watched a mare and foal together and it was obvious she craved having a foal of her own. Sally was beside herself in desiring to be a mom. She would pace back and forth at the mare and foal paddock, stretching her neck hard across the board fence to smell the scared little equine, who kept his distance from this seeming aggressor, by hiding behind his horse mother.

Soon, I found a rental house with some pasture and moved myself and Sally, but not the city boy husband. It quickly became evident that Sally was not happy in a field alone. Mules are social creatures and do much better when housed with or near a buddy or two.

On the bulletin board at the local feed store I noticed a hand written note about a 4 month old just weaned male donkey for sale. It was perfect. Sally's desire to raise a foal could nearly be realized and a buddy to pal around with to boot when he got older. Satchmo, the jazzy donk, came into our lives at that time. Sally and Satchmo became lifelong friends.

At a later time I went to visit with Zip and Candy. The wife was again pregnant and totally stressed out trying to handle her growing young family. The dairy farm owners expressed their desire to get the burdensome and costly monkeys (Zip and Candy) off their back. Being in a little better financial position, I gladly offered to take Zip home with me. The owner insisted that the two could not be separated. They were so bonded that the wife feared one would die without the other. The timing was perfect, as I had again moved and this time had much more land available to me. I was honored to take both equines home with me.

Fate created both Zip and Candy to come live the rest of their lives out under my care. Now I had four equines to care for. They all became a happy family—Zip/dad (32); Candy/mom (30); and the two kids, Sally (13) and Satchmo (2).

Candy passed on at the age of 34, and Zip graduated to higher realms at 37 and a half years young. My concerns over Zip leaving me after a few short years of acquiring him was unsubstantiated. He blessed me with his presence for 21 full years!

Zip & Candy, the Aging Horses, On:
Rejuvenation Of Life

This chat was held soon after I brought Zip and Candy to their new pasture and home with Sally and Satchmo. I had leased out 20 acres on someone else's family farm about a mile from my rental house in Lyle Washington. The family was very good to me and I appreciated them allowing me to bring two additional equines onto the property. On this day, I wanted to know how the newcomers felt; and if they liked their new home. I took pen to paper and asked them.

ZIP: We are alive again. Other horses, challenges, problems, make us feel like horses again, having to handle what comes up. You are here a lot and Candy is realizing that you are going to take care of her. She now is seeing you as someone that will help her. Her last people were nice but didn't help, really. She knows she will get the feed she has been missing and will get back to prime health. It is nice that someone is actively caring for us and keeping us in tip top shape. Some problems were getting me down, and I didn't feel I was being heard by the other person [at the last home]. So we just dealt with it.

You have lived a long time, both of you. What have you learned in your years?

ZIP: There is no need to move on (speaking of death) at this time. Both of us connect with the other side a lot. We live half here and half there. Sometimes these bodies are burdensome, but there still is more to do here. We have been waiting to get back with our person [Cindy], as our information can get out now. It couldn't with the other person.

CANDY: When an older horse enters your life, the person must change her perspective on a few things. Care is more insistent. Time is of the essence. Immediacy is important. This is not a job for a procrastinator. When we came here [Lyle] we had visions of going to heaven. Well, we still have our bodies, but someone to care for us and others to interact with is almost like heaven!

ZIP: I have one thing to say to all out there who care to listen to an old guy. Be kind to your horse and find that balance within yourself to be able to care for you and your horse both. If you have lots of animals, it will be essential to take the time for each and every one of us. If your other obligations are too much, please do not have any more animals than you can handle. Time, care, and financial means are important. When one gets over their head and cannot allow these for their horse, then all suffers, even the person. We see it happen over and over again. We horses help people with learning and practicing responsibility. A healthy horse is both a happy horse and a happy owner.

Candy, the Arabian Mare, On:
Dying is Okay

Candy was 31 years old at the time of this chat and had only been with me for about a year. Prior to Candy's stay at the dairy farm, apparently she had belonged to several folks through the years. This gal was an extremely good riding horse, but I didn't partake in that activity much with her, as Candy was plagued with arthritis in her legs pretty bad. Whenever Candy laid her body down to rest, it took a few humans to help her get back up on all fours. Candy's rear legs just couldn't lift that hind end like it could in her younger, stronger days. It became a panic situation each time I would find her down, wondering if she had given up on life and we wouldn't be able to get her standing again.

This unique morning I sleepily crawled out of my warm cozy bed to brave the cold outdoors, only to see my breath rise on that crisp fall morning. The nickering of hungry critters, in anticipation of satisfying an empty belly, helped me to wake up in a fine, loving manner. Out I meandered towards the barn to feed as usual. Three out of the usual four equine heads popped up out of the glassless windows in the barn.

Wiping the sleep from my eyes, I looked again. Candy was not in her usual spot to eat. "Oh geez, where's Candy?" That initial concern fully and immediately woke me up. Adrenaline rushed through my system as I quickly scanned the pasture, wondering if she was up, down, sick, or okay. "Yes!" I exclaimed as I saw her in the back pasture, standing on all fours. "Phew, at least she's up." Relief overcame the adrenaline, but something wasn't right as she wasn't at her usual breakfast-ready post.

Once our gazes met, Candy nickered to me to come get her. What was going on? Why wasn't she at the barn? I quickly grabbed the handiest halter and lead rope I could find and disregarded the other three equines' insistent plea to be fed. Out in the field I traipsed with the others literally on my heels. They were NOT going to let me forget they wanted breakfast.

On that autumn morning, Candy was all stiffened up on her legs and wouldn't budge an inch. She seemed to be hurting pretty bad, particularly on her left front leg. I donned her halter and after an exchange of trust, love, prodding, she insecurely began to test out movement. Once moving slowly and gingerly, Candy seemed to loosen up fairly quickly. We all walked around for a little bit and then headed back to the barn for that much anticipated breakfast. Once busily munching on hay (beautiful music to my ears), I had to ask Candy what happened for her to become lame.

I need to know from you, Candy, what's going on?

This old body just ain't what it used to be. I know it's been going downhill for quite some time. I feel the pains of the body. I would like to get out of this body. Sometimes I don't want to disrupt the flow of what we have here [the animal family]. We go in and out of our bodies, mentally. Quite often, Zip and I have one foot there (wherever they go after death) and one foot here [in this life].

The pain I feel. I got down (laid down) and had a hard time getting back up. When I got up, it hurt so bad, I didn't want to move. So I stood there. It was okay when I just stood. When that trailer came we thought we were going to heaven together, and that would have been fine. (The previous day I had moved the horse trailer around the farm). There is such a bond between us [her and Zip], that we both wanted to see each other through to the end. I don't want to leave him, he doesn't want to leave me. I feel more confident in leaving now that he has a friend he can stay with while I'm gone (speaking of Satchmo, the donkey and Sally, the mule). I don't work so hard on making my body work now. It's okay to go. I've had joy in the last part of my life. I again was family with other horses and animals. I, again, was with a herd. One is nice but a herd is much better. Much better for everyone's well being.

Candy On: Older Horses as Burdens

Another time I consulted with Candy regarding the wisdom of older horses.

Okay Candy, you have lived a lot of good years and have been with a lot of owners. Any thoughts you would like to say that you haven't said before?

We see people living their lives and being burdened by their horses. They are too busy, yet they are stuck with us. So, in their busy-ness, they cannot allow sufficient time and energy for us. But their attachment to us is not so much emotional, as it is responsibility. They are attached in a responsible way. And some emotional, I suppose, but they cannot properly care for us. I want to say what I have said before. That is, make sure you can afford us, time and money, when choosing a horse as your pet. As when we get old, we will need more of both. And there is no greater disappointment than being set aside because someone really doesn't want you, but they cannot get rid of you. We would rather die. I have stayed until Zip could be with others to experience these last moments of joy in a herd. I want to thank you for that. If you (speaking collectively) can see your way clear of giving old horses their lives back, you would make a lot of horses happy.

Candy apparently wasn't ready to leave this earth at that time, as she lived for another few years. We assisted Candy to pass on humanely at the age of 34, after a terrible fall and her not wanting to rise.

Satchmo, the Jazzy Donkey, On:
Getting Along with my Herd Family

Satchmo the Jazzy Donk is an interesting character. Not being as familiar with donkeys and their way of being living in a field of other equines, I was in for an education when I got him. The natural behavior of a donkey is different than a horse in many aspects. One of the most interesting is the pecking order syndrome.

When feeding horses, the strongest horse chases the weaker horses away from the food pan in an aggressive manner. The horse with the higher pecking status will do whatever it takes to be the only one at the desired feed bucket. The weaker horse, if s/he does not give in to the demands, is subject to being bitten or kicked until s/he gives the stronger horse full access to the feed. Once established, the weaker horse usually does not challenge his/her pecking order position.

Donkeys are a bit different. Since the pecking order is not as prevalent in donkeys, these longears don't interpret the horse chasing them from the feed pan as a pecking order action that they must never question, as it is with horses. I've watched Satchmo's behavior when it comes to feed time. He will allow the horses or mules to chase him away, to kick at him, and to bite at him. Satchmo will humor them and move away, but will keep coming back over and over again. Satchmo will keep pestering the higher pecking order animal until the horse (or mule) finally gives in to his constant insistence, and lets him eat from the same pan. This act is something that rarely happens in the horse world.

One day, as usual, I took my spiral notebook out to the barn to see who wanted to chat with me. Here comes Satchmo the Jazzy Donk. Satchmo is such a character and has a grand sense of humor. I was pleased he wanted to be the messenger of the day.

Take my hand and walk with me. You can see what I see from my vantage point. Being together is a vital element of comfort, contentment, happiness. Sometimes pets are in your [human's] life to bring you together with something, as there are difficulties in being together with humans. We show you the way to be in our state, which is what you want. You want to live in peace and harmony, as you see us live that way. We invite you to be part of our herd, but always know that your real herd is with humans. We can show you what an ideal herd is like so you have a goal to strive for in your human herd. Our friction is quick and immediate. Someone doesn't like something, s/he lets the others know, sets the stage for further communion/union. We don't hold grudges, we don't pretend, we don't hold back feelings. When I like the others, I let them know now. If they kick me, that is okay. I stated something, they stated something. If they didn't like me, I will get them to like me. I don't just go away forever. I have to be on the bottom of the pecking order, but I will get them to accept me, as I want to be with them. It feels good.

Satchmo On: Playing Well with Others

For three years I had a very special canine pooch, Cheyenne. Cheyenne and Satchmo would spend time playing by chasing each other back and forth in the field. Cheyenne would run after the donkey, barking to get his attention if he didn't immediately acknowledge her. Once agreeing to the game, Satchmo would lay his ears back and begin to chase the dog. Cheyenne would quickly skirt underneath the fence and Satch would go back to grazing. Scooting back under the fence, Cheyenne would then begin the barking scene again trying to get Satchmo to chase her. Satchmo would finally oblige and begin the chase one more time. This would please Cheyenne and she would escape just inches ahead of the seemingly aggressive donkey teeth. This time the German Shepherd turns on a dime. Satch isn't quite so quick to turn and runs past Cheyenne. Cheyenne turns around and entices Satchmo to chase her again. This back and forth play would go on for 20 minutes or more.

Personally, I didn't feel there was a problem with this, except I wasn't fond of Cheyenne's barking. For these two there certainly didn't seem to be any malicious intent with either party. Both the donkey and dog seem to enjoy it. I certainly don't recommend this activity for other dogs and equines. I understand that a dog is a predator and an equine is prey. This sort of playing could spill over into a category of instinctual chasing for the kill, so this activity must be monitored very carefully.

Satchmo had this to say about their chasing game.

We play, and we love to play. We have a relationship, me and that small thing. I like having one smaller than me and especially one that I can chase and she runs. (Laughs.) Sometimes I don't want to chase but she keeps after me. Sometimes I want to eat and I don't want to kick at her; but I do want to tell her that I don't want to play. She is getting to know and understand me. I don't want to hurt her. Most of the time she doesn't listen to me. She is into her play and wants that to continue and doesn't want to hear if I want to or not.

Zip, the Appaloosa Gelding, On:
Dogs Chasing Horses

Zip is a grand character. He is an old style, big boned, Appaloosa horse gelding. Zip's background was that he belonged to a friend of our family when we were growing up. This owner had quite a few horses and used them on a pack string with the U. S. Forest Service. As the gentleman aged, he sold off his horses one by one. Zip was his last horse, his favorite, and was passed down to his son, Kevin. Zip came to me at the prime age of 16. Kevin had decided to get totally out of the horse business and offered Zip to me. The minute I rode Zip I was in love with this dream horse, this push-button horse.

I used to watch a neighbor horse who would periodically be chased around the field by their owner's dogs. With Satchmo and Cheyenne enjoying their "field game," I felt a little confusion on how a horse interprets a dog chasing him, so I asked Zip about it.

Where does it come in that animal chasing animal in an aggressive way is okay and when is it not? A predator chasing prey in the wild is natural, the cycle of life. But in domesticity, it is not okay. I am trying to get a clearer understanding of that.

When a dog chases a horse, a horse will run out of instinct. The horse is very fast and can outrun a dog in the wild as we have many miles available to us and we can out-last the dog. In a pasture, we can only go around in circles or use our fight instinct and kick or bite—which is not as developed and we may not be as accurate, like a mule or donkey is. They are very accurate [kickers]. *They know* if they are going to hit or not going to hit. A horse sometimes isn't that accurate because we don't use that defense method as much. We kick out, rather than kick at.

So when your predator animals chase prey animals in a domestic situation it is not the same as the wild. Precautions have to be taken because the predator has many more advantages than the prey in the domestic situation. And [they] can hurt us without us willingly giving in. I don't know many horses who enjoy this and think of this as play. Actually, it is pretty irritating to us.

The donkey likes it because he plays too. We don't play that way. We have never played that way. It's not in our nature. We would rather run. And when we run, they chase and they bite our heels and our tail and they hurt. Sometimes they are mean and that is not what we care to partake in. We are very aware of dogs as they are predators and we are leery of them at first. When they prove to us they are no threat, then we can accept them. We do not mind them being with us when we are on a ride. They are more than welcome if they stay out of our feet. Those little yapping cattle dogs are the worst. They are so focused on instinct that they do not listen to us when we tell them 'no'.

Thank you, Zip.

Sally, the Wonder Mule, On: Animals as Models For Humans

My favorite buddy is Sally, the Wonder Mule. Sally and I have a special relationship. I bought her untrained at two years old and we learned together about mules. It's been a very bonding relationship ever since. Sally has always wanted a job, but I was unable to provide her with a consistent purpose in life. We worked on a few projects, including the pack string job, but nothing lasted as a regular job for her. Now Sally's job is simple. Our farm borders miles of desert land and we venture out for short day rides with other livestock following loose behind.

I've always said, "There is nothing better than being on the back of my mule in the woods". Sally will probably outlive me, as a mule's life span is from 30-35 years. I have had numerous chats with her, but most were not documented. On this day, I brought out my spiral notebook and sat down with her.

Sally, what do you want to talk about?

I want everyone to know how important humans are. They are the mainstay of society. We animals who choose to be around humans do so to help humans along the path of discovery.

It is my desire to share with humans that they can be more mule-like. As my person has observed, we animals are like the best person and it behooves you—I like that word, behooves—to model yourself after us. The main difference between humans and animals is ego, not brain, as they are led to believe. You watch us animals and we love, we play, we take care of ourselves in unity. We live our lives as you humans strive to live your lives. We are the ultimate. We want you to do as we do. We are the models. We are what you should be striving for. Can you see the value in humans that act like animals and also have a brain to make things happen?

I love you and it's okay I don't have a physical job. I have a mental job with you, this being one job [the communications]. But before you came along to this [mental] place, I was here to keep you focused on me and that I did want something. Trying to please caused you some stress/guilt but in the end you came to this, our conversations. Before we get too worldly or highly spiritual thoughts, I have to let the world know about mules. You have said all the appropriate words, yet it hasn't connected with many. What they learn about mules is not just about mules, but about other animals/pets and then about life.

Sally On: The Difference Between Mules and Horses

Sally, do you have something to say about the difference between mules and horses?

Just treat your mule as you would like to be treated. We are different animals than horses. Our method of getting through to you may not be like a horse. Study your mule and figure out what s/he is trying to tell you. If you expect us to act as horses, you will not understand us as well. Each mule will do what it takes to be heard. The more the human tries to determine what the mule is saying, the less obnoxious the mule needs to be to get through to the human. Mostly, we are trying to tell you something. Having only the horse for a point of reference, some humans will quit listening when the mule exhibits a behavior that is not horse-like. We want you to be sensitive, not only to mule communication, but to other animal communication as well. Our goal is to be at peace with you and try and get you to be at peace with us.

Sally On: The Historic Value of Mules to Humans

We have helped man to evolve. We helped him to use his brain. We had such high hopes for humans and their brains. But what happened was that the ego came in and took away all we had worked towards in helping humans to develop. They tossed us aside and we had to figure out a new way to help. Now it is 100 years later and back in further attempts to help humans out of their predicament. Going back 100 years we continue with the journey we were on at that time. Of course this time it's different. We must approach it from a different angle and show humans the benefits of being egoless, like us animals—for them to recognize how valuable play and friendship and unity with one another is. When we have problems, we are exaggerating the human problem to point it out to them. It behooves you to look at problems with us, as a problem with you. Fix that, and we are fixed. Simple. We just help you to grow.

Sally On: Laughter and Mule Tricks

Sally, how do you like being taught tricks.

Tricks are fun. They generally are things I enjoy doing anyway, and now I can do them and get paid (treats) for them. I like having that new skill and there is laughter when we do tricks. That pleases me, of course, as I join in on the laughter. Laughter isn't a common trait amongst mules. There is joy and peace and just being together in fight and play, but laughter isn't something we engage in. We get that from people. People laugh and that brings us joy. We don't have a way to smile, as that has not been needed from us. Other mules know when we are in peace or disturbed. We have ways of showing that. We also have ways of showing love. But laughter is a human thing, for the most part. And it is a pleasant thing. Cindy and I laugh together when we do tricks. She enjoys it and I play along. I know she wants to do the comedy routine, but I am just okay with doing a few tricks and getting away with them. In learning tricks, I am learning to manipulate things differently than if I hadn't been taught these tricks. Like, to open up doors, gates, and get out. Then when we trot down the street, we all are laughing! (Picture of Sally and Satchmo when they got out on the highway and were on their way elsewhere.) It is joyful to be free and mischievous. Don't ever give up laughter (speaking to humans). It is an outward expression of joy. And in its genuine state, there is no better way to express that inner pleasure.

Thanks so much Sally. I'll continue with the tricks, for both of our pleasure!

Neighbor Horse in Yard On:
I Want a Horse Buddy!

Living in Lyle, Cheyenne highly anticipated our daily dog walks to the Columbia River. The house I rented was in town surrounded by several other homes, as city blocks generally are. The small community of Lyle had a country atmosphere. A couple blocks down the road on the short trek to the river was a house with a small yard which housed a horse. This gelding seemed to have everything he needed: food, water, shelter. He acted as though he was not overly stressed out. Each time I saw him on our walk, I felt he wanted to talk but only today did I bring my note pad to chat with him.

Okay, gelding. You have been wanting to talk to me. Tell me, what do you have to say?

Sometimes I have things to say and no one to hear me say them. My owner is a fine man and cares for me but I need to be with other horses. It's like a human being isolated from other humans and only have animals around. That only works for some time. Pretty soon the human needs to go out and be with other humans. That is where I am at right now being a horse. I need to go out and be with other horses. Can you tell him to put me out with the other horses (speaking of my family of equines). I know it is a thought in his head. I want him to do that as I would feel better and I could run and stretch my legs if I was in a big field with other horses. He cares for me here, that is fine. I need to stretch my legs, it is very small here. I want to interact with other horses, too.

Okay, I will try to encourage him. And I will have others encourage him to put you out in the field with other horses. Anything else you want to say, Mr. Gelding?

No, that's about it. I want to go out to that field because I know you talk to all your horses out there and I want to put my two cents worth in when possible.

Thank you very much. I appreciate it.

(Shortly after, the owner agreed to put this gelding in with my animals and this gelding flourished in personality. He became good buddies with Satchmo the donkey, in particular. They drove each other crazy!)

Spokeshorse On:
Evolutionary Path—Amoeba to
Animal to Human

Sometimes finding subjects to talk about takes effort. On this day my mood was quiet and serene. I just didn't want to extend any extra effort. It was one of those fabulous cool spring mornings where I didn't have anything pressing that needed my immediate attention. I gathered up my trusty spiral notebook and fold-up lawn chair. Out into the horse field I wandered. Finding that perfect spot, I unfolded the lawn chair and settled in. In the sun's warmth contrasted with a slight chill of a definite breeze, meditatively I put pen to paper....

In the field with all the animals, the peace is so prevalent. I have no desire to speak, as voice interferes with that peace. The munching of the grass, the pulling up of the grass with horse teeth. The grass willingly being separated from its parts, knowing it's all a cycle and the grass will come back. Knowing that oneness is what it's all about. There is such peace. And now I know why being with animals is such a nourishing time for me.

It is my sanctuary to be out here in this quiet farm with chickens in the background and equines in the foreground. Lush pasture and budding trees in full spring renewal is the view from this lawn chair. I am quiet.

Quiet is my sanctuary. Quiet helps me to connect. Quiet is my heaven. If there is something I need, it is quiet. When the dog is barking, when the TV is intruding, when the radio is yakking, I am in my mind—my left brain, my thinking, reasoning mind. When I am quiet, I am in my soul, in the now. To hear my soul I need to have external sounds turned off. When I train horses I use very little voice. And people question that as it's unusual to witness. When I train it's soul to soul, just me and that equine.

It's a beautiful sunny day. Windy and a bit nippy, yet the sun is combating the wind and spring is here. I see the animals grazing and am thoroughly enjoying the view. Tell me (not specifically directed at any one being) how pets fit into the lives of humans.

When things evolve, when creation happens and souls evolve, there is some sort of a gradual order of evolution. And each order is more difficult to achieve—inanimate objects, live amoebas, small animals, large animals, apes, and humans. Some people believe that the evolutionary chain is better as you go along—that humans are the best. And that is not accurate. The evolutionary chain gets increasingly difficult.

As with any job you do, the higher you get on the corporate ladder, the more you have to work at it. You take all the experience of the other ladders and apply it to the one you are on, wanting to climb to the next ladder. As pets, they are one step closer to humans and one step more difficult in their job. As pets, they are one [rung] down from humans. It is easier to be a wild animal than a pet. It is easier to be a wild animal that has NO contact with humans than a wild animal that does have contact with humans. Each evolution brings up new challenges. And each evolution helps the next evolution. Every single being wants to evolve. Every single being wants others to evolve.

Why is it important?

Those that are further down the food chain, as you would say, know and realize we are all one. And their evolution and their brother's evolution create collective evolution.

So the further along the path of evolution, the more difficult it becomes until you get to humans?

Pets are more difficult because they have to overcome the closeness with humans. Pets are a very valuable state of being, as they can directly affect human beings. The path of the human is the most challenging as it is the one that has gone through the veil of forgetfulness and does not realize or acknowledge its connection with the Creator. Lower evolutionary matter and beings do [remember the connection]. There is no question. In animal to human relationship, the pet is a link between humans and those that know. Humans are drawn to pets because they [pets] are drawn to be connected. Every human being wants to remember and connect with the Creator.

And I also like to explain this Creator verses unity verses oneness [in a metaphor]. There seems to be some confusion here. In all of life, every being, every aspect, every blade of grass is a certain percentage of God and a certain percentage of individual (an analogy). From the grass, which is 99 % God and 1 % individual, to the birds which are 80 % God, 20 % individual. To pets, who are 60 % God and 40 % individual. To humans, who are 40 % God and 60 % individual. But in every one of these creations God is there. And the higher percentage of God, the more the being knows of the connection.

I have to speak of unity, of oneness. Oneness is the knowing of which percentage you are. The knowing of the percentage of you that is God. That is the 40 % that is God [in humans], is the 99 % that is God in a blade of grass—it is that awareness. For humans, they only see the 60 % of individual and because of that color of glasses they wear, they perceive the rest of the world to be the same percentage. They can only see out of their own eyes. That is part of the veil of forgetfulness.

Very insightful. Thank you so much for that perspective, Mr. Spokeshorse.

CHATS WITH WILD ANIMALS, BIRDS, FISH, & INSECTS

Once fluent with animals that we humans live our lives around, it just made sense that other living creatures would probably have a voice also. This first chat was spurred by a measure of desperation, as there was a problem I didn't know how to solve with sugar ants. Once successful, it really opened my eyes that other creatures of the planet had valued opinions, wise advice, and profound insights in which we humans are deaf. Here are some of those important insights.

Sugar Ants On:
Let's Make a Deal

As stated, a few years back I lived in Lyle, a small Washington town on the banks of the beautiful Columbia River. Lyle was a peaceful time in my life. For once, I only worked part time and I thoroughly enjoyed my off time. It was most precious being able to spend time doing just what I wanted to do. Living just three blocks from the local coffee shop, I became friendly with the morning coffee gang to satisfy my social need. My German Shepherd dog, Cheyenne, and I would go for walks down to the river at least once a day. I spent many hours having chats with any living thing that I could find.

In the warm to hot months of Lyle, sugar ants were prevalent inside the houses of the local residents. These hardy little ants would gather their organized selves and march confidently into the Lyle homes and businesses, subsequently eating everything they could get their tiny mouths on, preferring foods that contain sugar. The yearly schedule of these tiny ants was to arrive in force in the spring and then depart in the fall.

The first season living on the drier east side of the Cascade Mountains, I wasn't familiar with sugar ants and their overactive ways. My home must've been a gold mine for these little creatures, as they looted the cupboards and counter tops like it was a treasure chest of ant gold. Through the course of the summer this infuriated me to no end. The ants were in every parcel of food in the house, in the toothpaste, and filtered into any unsealed food canister. I ended up throwing out quite a bit of food that year due to their invasion. Subsequently, I learned that everything had to be in canisters and sealed containers.

After the first year ant disaster, the following spring I was determined to find a solution for the sugar ant problem. Asking around the coffee shop, most of the gang thought nothing of using readily available poison from the supermarket to keep the ant population to a minimum in their homes. Not wanting to take that deadly aggressive route, I wondered if I could actually create the sugar ants to not invade my home through conversation and reasoning. I knew that if they didn't oblige, I would have to use the poison to kill them as my last option. One warm spring day I took a walk with Cheyenne, settled myself on a rock wall near the river, and decided to carry on a chat with the sugar ants.

I will talk now to the sugar ants. I am open to you, ants. Can we work together on this problem?

We want to thank you for being kind enough to warn us of your intentions so clearly. If there is food out for us [dirty dishes and/or food on the counter] we will go to where there is food.

I have no problem with who you are as beings. I see your total focus. I love the way you all are part of one, no fighting amongst yourselves, no territoriality. You all are working in unison. I see that you have a definite purpose—one which I am not sure of, but it's obvious that you are focused on something. I just ask of you to not enter my home.

When you say "home", how far reaching do you mean?

Taken aback by their question, I had to think for a moment on where I would allow them to be and where I would request them not to be. (Thinking...)

The boundaries of the structure, the foundation, the interior, within my sight when I am inside the home.

It is our time of the year now. And since we reproduce quickly you need to restate this daily for all new ants being created. We have never worked with a human on this conscious level and ask for your cooperation.

The sugar ants then gave me a list of requirements needed to be able to satisfy my request.

1. Keep food away so we are not tempted.

2. Request this of us daily upon arising.

3. Value us.

4. Don't make a big deal out of this. Don't tell other humans, as that puts you in a different state [of mind] and not as conducive to this experiment.

Thank you, I will do all of these things and try and keep my ego out of it.

The feeling and thoughts I received on "don't tell other humans," was that quite often I would talk to animals or nature and brag about it to people. When that happened, my ego was in full force. I would tell others how wonderful and special I was by doing what others could not do. By conversing with these beings, especially when it comes to something I could interpret as power over them, I felt better than others. I could hear myself say, "I talked to the sugar ants today and they told me they would not come into my house." But the arrogant state that put me in actually would create the opposite to materialize—the sugar ants would start invading my house! The person I was bragging to would visit my home, see the ants, would then have fodder for disbelief and discount, and possibly be convinced that I was mentally crazy, highly weird, and/or making it all up. Not only would I alienate that person, but it would increase my chance of invalidating all my nature conversations.

Throughout that sugar ant season I held up my end of the deal as the ants requested; and they held up their end of the deal. My summer sugar ant problem was finally under control. Occasionally one would enter the house, but I would state my intention again and there would be zero ants for several days. I lost no food that season and acquired many colorful canisters plus a continually spotless kitchen! It is amazing how cooperative other beings are willing to be with us, under the right circumstances.

Baby Squirrel On:
God in a Shoe Box

It was 9:30 in the evening. The day had been busy and profitable as Portland's rainy weather usually brings in more taxi customers. My lease of the cab was until 11:00 p.m. I marked into the Marriott Hotel taxi stand to take a much needed rest. Fatigued by a busy nine hours of constant driving, I released the driver's seat to the reclining position and my eyelids became instantly heavy.

The taxicab company's computerized dispatch system allowed the dispatcher to send text messages to all drivers over a small computer screen mounted on the dashboard of the cabs. "Beep, beep" the computer squawked to signify an incoming message, disturbing my half asleep state. The dispatcher had sent an unusual all-fleet message. The screen read: "Anyone wanna do good deed?". Hm...What an interesting message. I figured the good deed would be a freebee ride for someone in need which would take me out of the queue, making me unavailable for paying runs. Should I respond? I contemplated the idea. It felt so good to rest my eyes and brain that I was inclined to disregard the message. However, curiosity got the best of me. I felt compelled to switch to the voice channel and just listen to the dispatcher discuss the particulars of this good deed to another driver's inquiry.

The story goes that two nice people had found an injured baby squirrel in their apartment courtyard and was kind enough to take him into their home to care for him. Being of gentle hearts but virtually penniless, these folks called the after hours emergency veterinarian clinic and asked if the on-call

71

vet would take a look at him for free. Apparently, the vet graciously agreed to donate his expertise on the hopeful rehabilitation of this squirrel.

Once veterinary help was secured, the squirrel finders conversation must have went something like this: "Okay good. The vet agrees to help him. Now, to get the squirrel down to the vet's office. But we have no car. Hm, how do we do this? Hey, I got it. Taxi drivers are all over town maybe one of them would come and pick up the little guy and take him across the Willamette River to the vet. Let's see now, what's the phone number for the taxi company?"

Even fatigued, I couldn't let this unique opportunity pass me by. I mustered up the energy and volunteered to do the good deed. The finder's address was about four miles from the Marriott Downtown. I gathered together my tired brain and body and headed my yellow cab east across the Morrison Bridge.

The folks in apartment C-3 on East Flanders Street were kind people, nice enough to wrap the little injured guy in a fuzzy washcloth and sacrifice a shoe box to be used for his bed. Niceties were exchanged between the couple and I. Soon I had this tiny sleeping squirrel in the passenger's seat of my taxicab.

In my careful travel to NW Portland's after hours emergency vet clinic, I purposely denied and ignored deep feelings inside that threatened to be revealed. I could feel myself suppressing a myriad of emotions. The timing was just not appropriate to allow them to the surface. Hey, I was on a mission. I had a valuable being in my cab. I had to pay attention to the road and all its turns and curves which could unsettle the important shoe box next to me. I had no time or use for these emotions right now. I held my emotional breath and focused on the vitally important task in front of me—transporting my customer to the doctor's office. The suppressed emotions were rising in my throat, and the desire to speak seemed to virtually disappear as I approached the clinic. Being aware that my window of opportunity was passing me by, I had to at least ask the squirrel for a chat. Maybe something that young and possibly sick or injured could not even communicate with me–I didn't know. Nevertheless, I choked down an obvious question to the sleeping infant:

Well, squirrel, you were brought into my life and that of the folks that found you, plus the vet office people for a reason. How come?

This little Godlike creature in the front seat of my taxi continued to sleep, yet stated one simple comment:

Look how you feel.

Just then the emotional volcano erupted. I became consciously aware of my repressed and denied feelings brewing just under the surface, which now couldn't help but burst forth. Immense honor and value came rushing in, filling my body. This was followed by high appreciation and sincere heartfeltness. This bursting dam revealed a matrix of sensitivities in which words couldn't adequately express. Some words that come close are: blessed, inwardly and outwardly proud in an egoless sort of way, totally worthwhile, a sincere, innate desire to help others in need, humbleness in the wake of grandness. I actually was shocked at the depth of emotion within but not allowed exposure until prompted by my passenger/angel/god.

This outburst of feelings rendered me nearly speechless and almost in tears, as I pulled up to the veterinarian's front door. I was working hard to come back to earth and be somewhat normal to the lady behind the counter. An overwhelm of humbleness was vividly apparent which prevented my eyes to meet one other chosen person of honor in this project, the receptionist. It was all I could do to place the little 'God in a shoe box' on the counter and wiggle out a quick and quiet "you know about this squirrel?" After a muffled "thank you," I scurried out the front door. Tears welled up in my eyes and escaped my cheek representing my heartfelt state. I felt exceptionally honored to be part of this experience.

Soon I was able to come back to reality. I gathered up my emotions, regrouped, wiped, blew, and headed out of the veterinarian's parking lot. The computer blurted another 'beep beep'. This time it was an offer for one last paying trip. I accepted with a new and powerful experience behind me. That seemingly innate object, the injured baby squirrel in the shoe box, assisted me to feel my own inner god, that unconditional love that is in all of us, in full force. What an emotional experience to end a great working day.

Squirrel On:
Cycle of Life or Murder?

What do you prefer to be called, a chipmunk or a squirrel?

A squirrel, as a chipmunk has meaning to humans that might not be desirable. A squirrel has desirable characteristics. A squirrel squirrels around and is able to get in and out of tight situations. And has abilities that maybe some other animals don't. And that is a better word for us. It is not such a bad connotation as "chipmunks" and the TV show [Alvin and the Chipmunks].

What is it that you have for us today squirrel?

Well, there are ground squirrels, and there are tree squirrels, and then there are squirrels that go from one to the other. I am one that goes from one to the other. I enjoy the ground and I enjoy the trees. I live in the ground for the most part as it is safer there. I don't have predators after me in the ground [that] I may have to deal with, as in the trees like other animals or birds. In the ground I'm pretty isolated, but I go outside for food, and I love to climb and I like going across the wires. It's like a tightrope walk. And we get pretty good at it. [Especially] those that do it all the time. For me right now I don't have wires to climb; but sometimes I do, I go inland and there are wires to climb.

So, what's it like being a squirrel?

It's a solitary life. We have a job to do. As the coolness draws in, the more urgent it is to do our job. This time of year [spring], we can play more. But we know where the food is and when it becomes available. And when it's ripe we do our job intensely. We are always looking to the future. We are unique in that respect. Many animals do not look to the future, they look to right now. We look to the future. And want to make sure we are going to get our [winter food] supply in.

What have you noticed in the earth changes, squirrel?

We do our job. We play. And we don't notice things to make a rational assumption or logic out of it. We see things, but just take them for today. You see things and worry about tomorrow. We only worry about our own survival. We have no idea what is to come, nor do we care. What we know right now is what instinct tells us to do. And if instinct tells us that we don't have to put our food aside right this moment, we play. It may behoove humans to think the same way. Too much outside influence leads to humans not listening to their instincts. Do what is in your heart. Do what you feel you need to do right now, today, as that will take care of tomorrow. Your instincts will guide you to be prepared for tomorrow in what it is telling you today. I have no idea what is going to happen tomorrow [nor] what has happened in the past. I don't care. I trust implicitly that when I feel an urge to put food away, that is exactly what I do, no questions asked, no comments, I just do it. That's just what we do. We are survivalists. We have been here for a long time. We have not had to use a rational mind to make sense out of anything. We just do what instincts tell us to do and that has created our survival. And that has prospered us for many years.

What about dogs and predators?

There is play in our lives. And one of the ways we play is through the chasing of us by another animal. There is a game that is played that is desirable to both animals. One chases, the other one runs. An adrenaline rush is in play. We get excited, they get excited, we win, they don't care! And sometimes a dog waits at the bottom of a tree for us. We go from tree to tree and the dogs can't figure out where we are (laughs) and that's our play. But the dogs enjoy it as much as we do. Every once in a while a squirrel is not capable of outrunning the dog. And in that case, it is okay. That squirrel has already agreed to be caught by the dog. Not in a conscious manner, but he just knows he doesn't want to run as fast this time. He does not want to 'squirrel' around as much and is willing to be caught by that dog. Judgment comes in, in human's eyes, and they say "Oh, that's awful. Kill the dog.

That poor squirrel". In actuality, this was agreed upon on a higher level for the dog to kill the squirrel. For the dog and the squirrel to play in this way.

I can't tell people that it's okay that dogs chase animals because I guess I don't believe it's okay. Here there is a game between a dog and a squirrel. And in this instance, there is an unwritten agreement that the dog will catch the squirrel. And that is okay in the cycle of life. But in our human world, it is not okay. In our world it a bad thing that the dog has caught the squirrel and kills it. So, I'm confused. When is it just the cycle of life, and when is it "murder?"

That is a judgment that humans put on [the outcome], not us squirrels. All we know is squirrel life. I will tell you what I know in a squirrel's life, and you will have to come to your own judgments in human life, and other animal life, or go ask those animals involved themselves. There is no murder in the animal world. That signifies that there are victims without any say in the matter. That is not so in either animal or human world. There has been a distortion in the human world. That which we do not fully understand, nor do we need to understand. I cannot say more on this, as it is not my business. That is the business of humans that needs to be resolved within. Just know, there is no murder in the squirrel world.

And squirrel, you have something more to say?

Just wanted to say that the fish your dog is eating is not good. (Cheyenne had found a dead fish on the beach while I was engaged in conversation with the squirrel.) I am here to talk to you if you want to converse more. I have more to say. I know it is a process in your time frame. I want you to know that I will be here to tell you more when you are ready for more from us squirrels.

Thank you squirrel, let me take care of the dog situation now.

Canadian Ducks On:
Unity in Flying in Flocks

You won't believe this, there are a whole bunch of Canadian ducks. I want to get close, but I don't want to scare them. (Counting)...there are 18 of them. I'm going to get close so I can talk to them. I want to sit down on this rock. Wow, every one of them has one eye on me.

Okay guys, I want you to know I am not a threat to you. You are gorgeous, you are beautiful. And I would like to sit and talk to you if that's okay. Please don't feel threatened, don't feel you have to fly away... So birds, what's your world like?

We know where the best spots are for food.

Are you going to fly off somewhere?

We know where the best spots for food are and go from place to place to place.

Do you always stay together as a unit?

When we fly into an area that has more ducks, then some go with other groups and some come with us. There is a group that flies, but it's not always the same group.

Are there consistent members of the group? Like do some go and others fall off? Or are there certain leaders that others follow, or what?

No. There are no leaders here. When a group of ducks decide to go, or when one duck decides to go, the others who feel like going at that moment will go. And the others will not. If one decided to fly [in this group now], we all would decide to fly because that's less danger. We are not a big enough group to split up.

How does the wind affect your travels?

Flying into the wind and having the wind on our beaks and our face and on our bodies makes it feel like we are surrounded and loved and enveloped into the oneness of all. When we fly with the wind, it is an added bonus because we don't have to work so hard.

What is it that you are eating here now? I see that you all are eating, except a couple of you are watching me. What is it that you are eating?

There are lots of bugs. Where there is dampness we have food. And here by the water we have food. You will see us flying by water quite often as the moisture brings the bugs that we eat.

How do you feel about humans?

They are an unpredictable sort. We stay away. We don't know if they are going to shoot us or talk to us. There are all variations in between.

Can you tell what their motive/intention is?

Oh yes. It's quite easy to tell. Ones will be more into themselves if they are out to kill us. There will be more attention outward if they want to embrace us.

Can I come closer?

A little bit. You can come to this knoll here. We won't fly off. But be gentle, we that are paying attention know your intentions. The ones eating may not and may fly. And if one flies, we all fly.

Okay, I'm going to try and come closer. I want you to know that I'm okay and that my intentions are clear—an outpouring of love for you guys.

Quack.

Oh, can you say something again?

Quack, quack. (from several ducks)

Thank you very much. You are very pretty. That white that is on the side of your head, how do you stay so clean?

In the water, we clean ourselves in water. Like our feet, they get cleaned in water.

I only have a little ways to go to get to the knoll. I have much value for you. Thanks so much for letting me be here with you. (Flock flies away). Oh, there they go. What's it like to feel that oneness? How does that feel?

Flying in unison. There is no leader, there is no follower. We all are a unit that meshes perfectly. There is security. That is why we do flock together— for the safety and security of each other. We all do what is necessary to survive, yet we don't have goals and dreams. We survive, we love, we play, we eat, we roll, we wash, we clean, and we groom ourselves. There is so much joy in doing all that. And then we do it all over again. That is the basis for our life. And it is a pleasant life. We are free to fly. There is generally an abundance of food.

Ever have sick or old ones that can't keep up?

Oh yes, there are some that when we are in a big group, they usually stay in the same area. While some fly away, others stay. And those are the ones who feel more comfortable in their own home area. They don't want to fly very far. They sometimes rely on people for food. It is their choice to do that, like in a park. Most of us are healthy and prefer to fly as flying feels good.

Thank you to the soul, the God, the oneness of the Canadian duck. Thank you so very, much for speaking with me and allowing me to speak with you.

It is our pleasure to find someone [who knows] who we are, how we feel, and to take a personal interest. We value and honor you, you are one of us. You are more one of us than you are one of them [humans] that we fear. We ask you to share your knowledge with others to bring them around to value and honor us. If they value and honor us and other animals they have to value and honor themselves more. Which will bring added peace into all of us— into the world. It will be a more pleasant place to be. We can all share this world, we just have to learn how.

Thank you, Canadian Ducks.

Pigeon On:
The Benefits of City Living

Living in Lyle, an easy means of transportation into the city of Portland was by way of the rail train. On the Washington side of the beautiful Columbia River runs Amtrak. This short one hour trip is a great leisure ride surrounded by pristine wilderness and follows the windy and mighty Columbia. The train travels the length of the Columbia River Gorge National Scenic area, the longest National Scenic Area in the United States. The Columbia River separates Oregon state from Washington state. In an hour's travel the landscape changes from barren, brown, treeless hills of the eastern side of the Cascades to lush gorgeous, evergreens and the fresh new leaves of deciduous trees of the western part of the state. I swear, this MUST be the most beautiful area in the country.

Amtrak just happened to stop in Bingen—a small town about 10 miles west of Lyle—in the morning and return in the early evening. This made it perfect for a local resident to spend a day in the city of Portland visiting old friends or partaking in a bit of shopping.

On this particular Sunday morning I boarded Amtrak in Bingen. This trip was to include attending a church in the downtown area of the Portland along with shopping and visiting friends. With settling in to the soothing side to side motion of rail travel I curled my legs and cozied onto a warm cushion facing a side window on this luxury trip. Caressing my styrofoam cup of Earl Grey tea, meditating with the gentle rocking, I absorbed the beauty of the clean, blue river, the deep green of the forest, and the lush vibrant hills as we rolled by.

It wasn't long until this pleasant experience was coming to an end. Portland was drawing near which was the end of this line. All fellow travelers began gathering their belongings anticipating the next phase—either waiting for a future train, or meeting their loved ones at Portland's Union Station. For me, I exited the train and had a leisure opportunity to mill around the city for about an hour before the onset of church services. Many retail stores were closed on this Sunday morning, so I began looking for something to occupy my time. I viewed a pigeon eating potato chips off the sidewalk and sat down on an artist's decorative rock to have a little chat with this city bird.

So, pigeon, how is life in the city and why do you prefer city living?

More food. Just as people gather in areas where all conveniences are nearby, all our conveniences are nearby too. We have much noise in the city and sometimes our calls have to be louder than at other places to be heard over the traffic roar. You would not believe the food available to us in the city.

So, tell me about homing pigeons. Are some of you that way or do all pigeons have a tendency to know where home is?

We all are that way. A city pigeon stays nearby throughout her life. It is her home. We do not fly south for the winter or leave. We stay. Taking us from our home we will come home, just like humans. Some choose the life of the homing pigeon, as humans choose to be in the spotlight and desire competition sports. Some pigeons desire to work more closely with humans for more effectiveness.

Effectiveness? Of what?

We all are in this process to aid humans to grow. It's like a child on a swing—push, push, and the child becomes more confident and wants to go higher. We ALL do the pushing to make you go higher! As it is fun for everyone. And, as the youngster in the class that is not as smart or as far long as the rest of the class, the other students want to help him along as he is holding back the rest of the class. You humans are holding the rest of the class back. That is why we assist you.

So, we are not as smart or as far along as other aspects of nature, animals and birds?

It's a different ball game as you have more in your head to get straight than the rest of us. Like if a Spanish [speaking] child was to enter an English [speaking] classroom, that child would have begun several steps 'below' the rest of the class and may need assistance to catch up. Not to say she was not smart, just beginning at a lower level as the other [English speaking] children.

Thank you, pigeon. I appreciate your insight.

Featherless Bird On:
Inner Power

Below is a request that came in from a woman. She wanted me to see what her bird with no feathers had to say. She stated:

"I have a baby bird sitting next to me. So tiny it has no feathers. It's very strong and very scared... It happened into my life at a time when I find myself spiritually challenged (loss of connection to my gifts). This bird is dependent on me to survive. Do you think this is significant? Anyway, if it's possible that you send out positive energy in my direction to help my little friend, do you think you could do that? I'd really appreciate it."

I thought I'd just let the bird talk.

I have entered your (collective) life to show you that as a person you have all abilities needed to assist or crush someone's life. You are gifted. Just as I am vulnerable and dependent, every human life is just like me, only not as obvious. Every human life is vulnerable and easily crushed. It is up to the empath who sees the lack of feathers and nourishes the human being until s/he has feathers and can fly on his/her own. What you all don't quite get is the vulnerability of humans. What you do with this gift is nourish or crush. It is up to you. Let me be a symbol of how you are to handle humans.

(Taking this information personal...) But I don't want to be the one responsible, here. I don't want my actions/words to crush another.

You are there already, my friend. You have been given this gift, it's up to you to do with it what you choose. How are you going to use it?

83

Oh geez. I guess I got to realize how deeply my actions affect others. I don't want to do that. I don't want to be responsible for another's feelings. Why can't I just be me and let the chips fall where they may?

The chips have fallen, but it is YOU that is complaining about where they are landing! Personally, I don't care where the chips fall...but you seem to! So, your inside hurt is their inside hurt. When are you going to stop hurting yourself? That is my question to you. My love to all of you along this empathic path. I honor you and your gifts. It is time to go now. Thank you for listening.

Signed: The Featherless Bird.

Even though this bird addressed my personal concerns, he also did address the owner's concerns. I presented this little chat to show one more profound bit of information that can apply to many readers.

Bird On:
The Urgency to Nest

On one of my many walks to the Columbia River and sitting on a favorite log, I began observing a bird that seemed to be in a nest on a man-made platform out in the water. The sun was low in the sky, directly behind the scene and it was difficult to decipher exactly what was happening in that nest. So, I decided to talk to the bird.

I think you have something to say, bird. I can't see you very well, as the sun is in my eyes, so therefore I don't know what kind of bird you are.

I am a nesting bird. I like to nest. I am here above my nest watching over it. I am looking at all the things in the sea [the Columbia River] and making sure my nest is protected.

So, not being sure of what kind of bird you are, what do you do in the course of a day?

I fly around and protect my home. I stay fairly close to my home. Soon, there will be eggs here and I will hatch the eggs and then my job is to raise my children. Right now, I have found my nest and I am protecting it in anticipation of what's to come.

So, when I come out here I should see you fairly frequently?

I will be in the area. I don't have to be right at this point at all times. It seems to be a good nest. From where I am perched I can see many directions for quite some distance to see if predators are around.

What is it like to fly?

We are a solitary bird. We generally don't fly in flocks. We have our lives to live and we live our lives. And flying is our form of transportation. It gets us from point A to point B. We go, we eat, I get twigs, I bring it to the nest, I build my nest.

Nesting seems to be in the forefront of this bird's thoughts.

Do you play?

Right now, I build my nest. There are times when I play, although I cannot recall them, as building my nest is what I do now.

Is building a nest a fun or not so fun job?

This is what I do at this time. I build a nest. I lay the eggs. I hatch the eggs. I feed the children. The children then go away and then I have freedom for some time until next time I build a nest.

So, what do you use to build the nest?

Twigs. As you can see, I have a very big nest. It is like a mansion in your terms. It was built by another bird, most likely. And I have found it and will make it to my specifications, kind of like remodeling a house.

How far are you along that process?

I have it mostly completed. I can make it better. Depending upon when it is time to lay the eggs. I will just make it better and better and bringing more twigs and things in that seem to be fine for the nest. The urgency of getting and finding a nest is over at this moment. I did find an adequate one that I can use.

What about the sound you make?

I get attention to other beings, birds. I tell them this is not where they need to be. That this is where I am at. I have gotten this nest. I warn animals to stay away. I don't sing for joy like some birds do, I sing as my purpose in building a nest and being in a "mother" state.

I want to thank you for talking to me.

Squirrels can raise havoc to nests that are in trees. It is very beneficial to find a nest that is over water, and not accessible to those darn squirrels (the bird laughs).

Raven On:
Soaring to Bless the Earth

I saw a crow or raven this morning. I would like to talk to him/her now. Hello, are you a crow or a raven?

Different words for the same. Some folks, such as Native American Indians, value us and call us "ravens". It seems they like that [word] better. Those who dislike us call us "crows". There is a meaning [or a thought] behind that, but I don't know what it is. Just that it is not favorable or valuing our worth. To humans, crows are a nuisance. To humans, ravens are special, valued, and honored.

Ok, Mr. Raven. I see many of you in these parts. I think you are beautiful. What do you have to share today?

When a human comes upon a raven, many changes are or have been occurring. We signify change. When a raven is in your midst, we glow as the moon on a full night. We soar, we bless the earth. We value the earth. It is our livelihood, our source of survival and pleasure.

Raven, this doesn't seem real. I just don't feel bonded to you.

When info comes into you that can be verifiably proved wrong, your walls go up and it restricts the flow of communication. Many levels shut down.

I had to admit that when the raven said that crows and ravens are the same thing only with a different name, my walls did go up. Here was a fact that I wasn't sure was a truth and could be proven wrong. The raven was certainly right about that!

Raven On: Enemies and Friends

At another home, in a place where ravens are in abundance, I got to know some ravens that hung around my little farm. What message would you like to share with us humans, Madam Raven?

Just as you have your home and enjoy it, we have our home and enjoy it. We have nests, and territories, and deal with predators, just like you. Sometimes they are easy to handle, like your dogs (one raven likes to tease the dogs) and some it takes more to keep us safe and protected, like you are with your coyotes. Coyotes don't bother us much. We know how to be safe around them.

Humans get very confused as to what is enemy and what is friend. We see them be fooled a lot of the time. Then they get mad because a particular person is not what they say they are. The problem is that the person getting mad could not tell who the opposing person was. They relied too heavy on words and promises and wanting someone to be a particular way. When we ravens come up against a bird who attacks and pesters us, we know it and deal swiftly with it. We don't allow the other bird to fool us. We are too aware. It would be wise for humans to develop their awareness so they won't be fooled by who is predator and who is friend.

Thank you Madam Raven.

Raven On: Dying to Re-emerge

One day as I was working in the yard, Mr. and Mrs. Raven were at their usual post, on the top of the electrical pole and wires. I noticed one of them struggling on the wire and then falling off of the wire onto the ground where he flopped around a bit and then lay still. Mrs. Raven watched over him as he struggled to survive. She even made a strong point in diving after my dog who had gone to investigate. Mrs. Raven stayed on the power pole for all day long. Several hours later, Mr. Raven began flopping on the ground again. Confused, as I figured he was dead, I went out and noticed he was still breathing even as he lay upside down at the base of the power pole.

Mrs. Raven watched over him into the next morning, where he still lay on the ground, alive and breathing. I had to have a conversation to figure out what was going on.

Mr. Raven are you dying?

I'd like to, but my wife is holding me here. She doesn't want to go on without me. We are like grandpa and grandma in your terms. We have been together for quite some time. But it's time for me to move on. But I can't move. I'd just as soon shed this body and re-emerge anew.

Mrs. Raven did you hear Mr. Raven's comments?

He has done this before. It's like a stroke in your terms. I'm not leaving until I know for sure that he is not going to revive. Then I will go on. We are a good team, a good match. We do love each other. I'm not afraid of him dying, I just see that he is not dead yet. And if there is a chance of him coming back, then I will be here. I won't abandon him. If I have to start a new life, then so be it. But if I don't have to, then I will wait for him.

Do you realize that you may be keeping him from moving on?

I am in waiting mode. Don't put blame on me. I am not responsible for him. You humans are a strange sort. You are into blame of self and others. The only one you have responsibility for is yourself. I am not holding him, I am waiting for him to decide what he is going to do. I want him to have the best opportunity to live as is possible, that is why I watch over him. But it is his decision. I will be fine either way.

Thank you, Mrs. Raven. And Mr. Raven, I hope you can move on peacefully now.

When I returned home from work that evening, Mr. Raven had stopped breathing. Mrs. Raven hung around my farm for a while longer. After a couple of days she moved on to a new life.

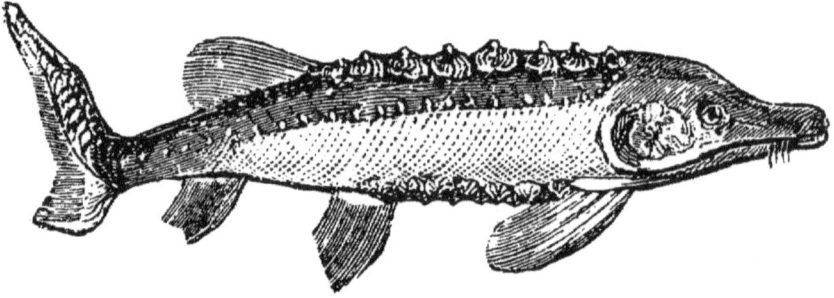

Sturgeon Fish On:
Bigger is Better?

At a fish hatchery on the banks of the Columbia River there is a grand floral display and a park like area with many fish in the huge tanks. In that hatchery, the star of the show is a very long and large sturgeon fish that must measure 6-7 feet in length. He is amazing to view.

So, Mr. Sturgeon, tell me about life in this fish hatchery for you.

We are here for humans to gawk at. "My how big they are." They think big is better. What they don't know is that I would not make it very long in the wild. I have never had to run or move fast due to danger. I would be caught or eaten quickly as I do not have the teachings of my brothers—the "street smarts" as you may call it. It is good that we are a distance away from people, through water. It protects us from their personality. Being around people is what we do. Sometimes they [hatchery visitors] feed us, most of the time they do not. If I, the big one, gives them attention, they enjoy that. I am cautious of their 'joy'. Sometimes it is mean intended. (I received the picture of boys squirreling around, showing off to others, projecting negativity to the fish.) Occasionally one falls in [the pond] and we scatter. Their smell and presence permeate the water for a long time. Pollutes it, if you will.

Thank you for your wise words, Mr. Sturgeon.

Salmon Fish On:
Honoring Us or Selfish Greed?

Right now, I'd like to talk to all the fish in the Columbia River. Hi fish! Is there any one of you who wants to be a "spokesfish"?

Oh, yes. There was a salmon caught here recently, a very large salmon. This salmon was similar to an Indian chief. This salmon had many wise words to say to all of us, as we are not quite so old and wise. We miss the salmon tremendously. We have absorbed what this salmon has to tell us, and he said you were coming. What he had to impart to all of us *was* completed [prior to his being caught]. The cycle was ended. We gathered around as we knew his time was near to go and we honored and valued him as he left. The community of salmon is very strong. There is a unity amongst us and we are more evolved than many of the other fish here. Even the sturgeons aren't spiritually concerned. We are.

We understand the problems humans have and we do our part to bring to the surface these problems, so humans can work with humans to resolve issues. We see a difference in native and white American beings. The native Americans have a gentler nature during the day and fall apart at night. The whites are crass during the day and crass at night. The message that we send is to create the turmoil that has been going on between the native and white fisherman. It has created the turmoil of dams. We have aided the creation of many difficulties.

If humans were going to ignore us, we would not be speaking. But some humans are listening. And in that are the natives. In the daytime, their [native Americans] lives are pro-fish, and pro-nature, and pro-animals, and pro-God. We create difficulties under the surface to bring out the attitudes of everybody in order to resolve some issues needing to be looked at to all humans. If we would swim around like the little fish around here and not create turmoil, we would all get caught and ate. There is an abundance of them, there is a minority of us. The difficulties that we find with humans is the gentle balance of nature. We are proud to be part of this process. As this ongoing difficulty keep laymen aware of the difficulty, of natural balance verses greed. The natives help with that process. Natives fight for honoring us. White Americans fight for money and greed. If we did not exist and were not endangered, the whites would win. The difficulties that we have, being a small group, is exactly what needs to be in the forefront of the white American's mind. Any animal/fish/nature that is becoming threatened is a call to the white American, is a call to the greedy, that they cannot continue without severe consequences. Now, the greedy is not necessarily the only ones.

Thank you for your words, Mr. Salmon.

Rattlesnake On:
Territoriality

At one of the most crisis-filled times in my life, the only good thing was that I purchased a six acre piece of land outside of Lyle Washington. This aided me to get away from the city of Portland with hurtful, angry people, and the hell I had just been drug through. The property I purchased was extremely sloped much like goat country—with a year round creek at the bottom. Sally's (my beloved mule) job was to haul water up the hill for me, as I had parked a camping trailer on a tiny flat spot, but had no water, electricity or septic system. This minimal facility stay was short-lived, but sufficient to begin my journey into a new life separated from the difficulties I had been experiencing in the city.

Being from the west side—the wet side—of the Cascade Mountains, I wasn't very familiar with rattlesnakes and dangerous reptiles that one may come across more frequently east of the mountains, near Lyle. On this peaceful welcoming property, I would occasionally run across a rattlesnake. I knew where "Rattlesnake" hung out and respected that area, as those rattler sounds triggered many western movie scenes. It was a special day when I sat down to have an insightful chat with him.

I would like to take this time to connect with the rattlesnake that is on my property. How do rattlesnakes fit in this world and what would you like to say?

We are not here to harm anyone. We have our life to live and we live it. We will only strike out of defense. If a person such as you talks to us and tells us that you appreciate and value us, then we appreciate and value you, and we can keep our distance. I don't mind having humans around, as long as my habitat is not invaded and I have to move. Like, if someone is to build a house and [begin] excavating, I would have to move down the hill to a better area where I would be less bothered, where I could have my food. My food depends on natural animals and things moving past. If there is human intervention, then not as many animal and nature things will walk past. I like my place here. It is peaceful and I have no fears, as no humans are around. I can sun myself without fear of getting shot. The only time I would strike is if I felt I was in danger. I rattle to 1. tell you where I am, to keep your distance; 2. for you to know where I am and bypass me. And 3. this is my territory and do not want humans excavating on it. You were kind enough to explain to me who you were and what you're intentions were towards me.

What about the people who are on the neighboring property?

They are there. I don't go there. They have no awareness of my value. I have plenty of room in this area, I don't need to be in their area. We leave each other alone.

Do you feel they would harm you if they knew about you?

Most certainly. They have that mentality. As do most people. Very few have your mentality.

Now, if I sell your home (my land), and the new owner begins excavating, how can I make it better for you?

I have been here for quite some time. I know the ropes. I know what's going to happen. And I know what food is available. And I know where to get what I need to live and eat. It depends on the person whom is on the ground also. If the person is down the hill in the center of the land, it will not bother us. And although it will be uncomfortable for a while through excavation time, I will not move from this land as it has everything I need. If he builds on top of my area, I would have to move. I don't think that's going to happen.

It wasn't long until I found a rental home in town and returned to living a 'normal' life with indoor plumbing, telephone, and electrical services.

94

CHATS WITH WATER, TREES, WIND, NATURE, AND THE MOON

If I could receive messages from many living creatures, what about nature things that are alive, but not really creatures? What about those things we encounter in life that have an aliveness that maybe we don't quite recognize in the same way? The trail blazing continued onward and inward to those more subtle, but certainly alive, beings.

Pine Tree On:
Being a Christmas Tree

I had some idle time before attending a business meeting one day at a local hotel banquet room. The foyer had a long cushy bench seat and I decided to utilize my spare time by writing. I dug a spiral notebook out of my briefcase. Looking outside the full length glass window, I spotted some tall pine trees. I had never tried talking to non-breathing type beings before. Hm...I wonder if pine trees have voices. It's worth a try. Surprisingly, the trees came through loud and clear.

We develop pine cones. That is our way to flourish on earth. The seeds drop and new trees are on the way. It is a unique idea to have the seed in such a complicated package. Look at the maple tree and the maple seed that airplanes down to the ground—a unique method of reproducing. We do say trees have more personality than you think. Not just in our voices, but in our style of living. Look at our branches. We have many. So many that there is not enough light for the inner needles. That is unique about pine trees. We are here to grow and flourish even in dire weather and dry, barren ground. We have the ability to search for our moisture through roots to keep us alive. Rarely does one see a pine tree dying of thirst. We enjoy the company of other pine trees. We can stand alone also, and will grow to grand size. We prefer to grow together in unison with other trees, even if we must share the sun. Those humans who gather under us, do so with pleasure whether we are one or many. If we have provided a cushion of needles, our visitors have a comfortable sitting area beneath our limbs.

What about Christmas tree farms and the pine trees grown for that?

[In tree farms] each tree is grown individually for the benefit of humans. We [forest pine trees] grow in unison for the benefit of ourselves. If humans grow us individually in rows never touching other trees, we do grow in more space and are more desirable for humans to cut down. This is not our preferred method of growth. Growing in groups pleases us most as our communal lifestyle prevails; all mixing and intermingling in an equal harmonious way, never choosing to part.

What about being used as Christmas trees?

The one benefit of growing alone is that when we are cut because a human likes us, we feel appreciated, valued and loved in our ending time. It is a pleasant way to go. It also is interesting to be that close to family and experience human lives for our end times. We are not able to reproduce during these times (people remove our seeds, no ground to germinate in) and that is sad. Mostly, we enjoy human interaction when in houses, as we are appreciated and kids love us and decorate us wildly. This is not our preference but we enjoy the enthusiasm from everyone participating.

Thank you for listening; and share with others to keep our home free of papers and cans and things we cannot dissolve into our soils easily.

I will. Thank you, Mr. Pine Tree.

Maple Tree On:
Oneness

Down at the Columbia River, a developer had cleared out an area to sell plots of land to build homes. To my benefit while living in Lyle, political and legal issues had delayed further development of this area and therefore it posed as a park for the locals to enjoy. Right smack in the middle of all this clearing, the developer left one very old, extremely large, majestic maple tree. This tree is so unique in its trunk, branches, and foliage that it is no wonder the developer left it standing.

I would like to talk you, tree, if I may.

The most that I can tell you/teach you/remind you is what you have already discovered today. Today you were me. You were an aspect of you being expressed by me. And that is all these chats are trying to do is to put people in other being's bodies to show we all are one. Yes, I am you expressing you, and you are me, expressing as humans. We are all one. And every animal and every tree and every branch and grass is one, being expressed in a slightly different way. And it's not necessarily for understanding, it's for unity. I think you are getting the picture. And I think that all your chats seem to connect humans with whatever you are chatting with. And with a slight and gentle way, you are telling folks that there is unity, that we are not all that different. That we are one of the same. We value and honor your process. And word is to get out to everyone. So everyone, at one moment in their lives, can feel themselves through a tree—to look at a tree and to be the tree. Because they are the tree, and the tree is they. And it's not that hard to do in that exercise …to expand and be other things just for a moment. And what you will find is a 'wow'.

It's not that hard to be a tree. If it's not that hard to be a tree, then humans and trees must be closer than [you] thought, and there lies our experience with you. If we can become one, the rest of the problems will solve themselves. I am a unique looking tree to draw your attention because I know you are partial to trees—and that you listen to trees and chat with me in a very succinct way. As you chose me amongst all the other trees to chat with, I am here for you. May this be your need to grow and bring [together] other people. Even if you are afraid of saying things that may turn people off, such as talking of unity. Your being, your personality, your thoughts, are relayed to them even if no words are spoken. People are much more willing to listen to a happy person than an unhappy person.

(Laughs.) You're good tree, you're good.

We will tackle these problems one by one. Right now, your chats [are] of uniting humans with everything else—with not feeling so separate. So have confidence in your chatting and continue them. You have a format now. I would like to see that expanded. I would like to see your voice expanded, too. Don't be afraid to talk about it. There is a deep part inside of every being that knows you are right when you talk of unity. And they may fight you, and they may ridicule you, and they may do things that are not pleasant. But to be true to yourself, you need to speak truths and they will come around.

I cannot thank you enough, tree.

City Tree On:
Human Development versus Happiness

Driving taxicab in Portland, my business man passenger said he needed to go to a particular office building in Beaverton, the next town west, for an after-hours meeting. The agreement was that I would wait for him, meter running, for just a few minutes of this short meeting, and then return him to his office in Portland as quickly as possible. We arrived at the Beaverton office building per the business man's request and the taxi meter continued to click over while the customer disappeared into the doors of the building, which slammed and locked behind him. The short meeting became a long meeting. "Just a few minutes" had passed and it looked like I may be there for a while. Dang, I didn't get money up front to hold me (to ensure his return). "What was I thinking? I've got to learn to not trust so fluently", I scolded myself.

Since I obviously had time to kill, I began noticing my surroundings. I was struck by the beauty of the trees and landscaping that was strategically placed in this fairly new business complex. I decided to have a chat with this one particular tree which was somewhat separate from the other trees. The deciduous leaves were rustling and provided entertainment for my waiting, bored mind. The trunk of this tree was totally surrounded by cement walkways on all four sides.

Beautiful tree, you provide such peace and majesty and beauty to this area—you and all your tree friends. Tell me, how do you see life from your viewpoint?

Once there were many of us [at this location]. We loved, we flourished, we swayed to the winds, all in unison. Slowly, the tight oneness and bond became less and less as trees were replaced with stuff that forever squished our floor [cement, asphalt, buildings], which seemingly were much more important to humans than we were. Where we used to have frolicking, we now have darkness. The dark side of humans who weave in and out of us [trees] who are left. You just don't know the difference when one tree used to be many trees. A part of me is sad in that it cannot touch other trees, as touch is joyful and connection. You will find that trees love to touch other trees and are not as healthy when separated, as that is not our nature.

But look at the beauty of a lone tree.

For the human who unthinkingly tore down my companions, maybe. Neither did they honor us or care about us. The thoughts in their heads [the construction workers] was not joy, but focused and uncaring. This is what we see from our tops looking down at humans walking past—focused and uncaring or unappreciative of us. Occasionally one, such as you, values us, recognizes us, but that appreciation does not make up for my ailing health due to seclusion.

Is there anything I can do for you?

Tell them my roots are cramped. Tell them I may die if not watered properly as my roots cannot reach for water like they used to do. Tell them we are sad.

Tell WHO?

[Tell] the people who don't care about us—the excavators, the planners, the developers. Sadly, we must share our existence with dark beings who will destroy us with no hesitation—for what, money? The dark side remains, no matter how much money they have or how many trees they destroy. Trees could make them happy, but instead they do away with us for money, as the [seeming] road to happiness. But it never works, anyway. Learn from this, too. Please share this to spare us. Thank you.

In this conversation a clear picture story was sent to me from the city tree. It was a story of humans seeking happiness. Their attempt to obtain happiness was through constructing buildings for eventual money/income. They would wipe out trees and earth, substitute cement and buildings, and realize their goals when the money came rolling in. These well intentioned but unaware folks did obtain money, but never reached their true seeking—that of real and permanent happiness. When in truth, if those same people would have put down their architecture plans, gotten off their destructive bulldozers, and went and sat under a tree, they would find that true, permanent happiness of their desire.

The businessman's time was up, as was mine. It was time to get the cab back to the office so the next driver could begin his shift. I attempted to go inside the building to track the guy down but the office doors were locked. The meter read $43 when I realized I had been duped—stiffed. The guy probably never intended to return to the taxi. It was one of those costly education runs. I took my losses, my pride, my city tree chat, and headed back to Portland.

Bamboo On:
Quit Being so Rigid, Bend a Little!

Being a lover of bamboo, I took the opportunity to go visit a small grove of various species of bamboo grasses that banked a small stream in Washington Park Arboretum, Portland Oregon. It was a peaceful, loving afternoon. I took pen to paper and had a chat with the bamboo.

Wow, you sound so sweet when the wind rustles your hair—a quietness about you. You do companion with water and a stream very well. What insights and wisdom do you have for me, bamboo?

We are a little patch amongst many trees. This is nice and we understand the purpose. But we are at our majestic when, for as far as the eye can see, we are there—that is, when we really come into our own. Our roots attempt to be all we can be. We have that capability and are not hampered or held back by little menial obstacles like humans, and like flowers, and like other trees who don't care to make a grove. We flourish when weaker gives way. Humans get irritated with us being "out of control" and invent many ways to control bamboo. If you look at those people closely, you will see they fear themselves to be out of control and generally wouldn't want invasive bamboo in their yard. Those that do, either have no inner control issues going on or severe control issues going on. How they react to our spreading is unique to the learning/growth of some individuals.

Maybe we create neighbor problems. People react to our spreading in their own way; and have us [bamboo], sometimes, to bring their own control issues to light so they can be healed. Those who don't fear spreading have ultimate control–and we can challenge that. Just let us find the weak link to their barrier! Or they just do their best and handle the problems of growing us in neighborhoods. If you are aware, you will see that the "problems" with bamboo spreading is a human/human thing. You are worried about lawsuits, money, territorial, control, acceptance, approval between humans. Given to our own devices, we are not as out of control as it seems. We co-exist with the rest of the forest. They don't seem to have "issues" around control.

You don't know us in our own habitat. You may never. We bring in many birds, animals, insects that are not in this environment. All co-exist and these critters feed and benefit from our grasses. We love it when they do. In controlled marketable groves, it misses this vital link. We still are happy and content, we just are a bit more out of our element. All is well, but if you can, get to a natural China bamboo grove (or other countries). You will know what we say.

One more thing—any plant, tree, shrub that is planted and loved is a stronger plant, as is the person doing the loving. If the person can feel our peace, the person is stronger, too. We love you and thank you for caring and always remember to BEND a little instead of being so rigid! Contrary to humans' popular belief, one is much stronger when they bend with the wind of life.

Thank you so much, bamboo.

Forest Fire On:
Being Out of Control

There is a forest fire flaming wildly on the hillside just on the Oregon side of the Columbia River.

Fire, do you have a message for us?

The question is 'do you have a message for the fire?'

Well, fire, I see that you are beneficial. You cleanse the ground and enable new growth. I see the benefit in fires. Some people don't. The people who work with you directly see your value too. So to the small bit of population who think you are a disaster, can you change their mind about this?

People will see disaster if that is what they are looking for and want to experience it, for whatever reason. It is not my place to place judgment on if we are good or bad. As that is in the eyes of the beholder. As you have witnessed, many people gather to watch. These gatherings are a way for humans to unite—to become friendly, to TALK to each other. If this is our purpose to many, so be it. Humans must unite for their own good. Uniting people with people aids in increased worth for all around, and this will spill over to nature of course. Now, don't go setting fires. We are aware that there are people [arsonists] who live to be given an excuse to do things they shouldn't do, and then justify it by saying, "someone told me to—told me to set this fire. I'm doing this to better people, don't you know?" That is bunk. Everyone knows that. The brain behind that voice knows that they have an out, a way to blame their behavior on something else. They have not fooled anyone. We ALL are aware of their doings.

Fire is necessary for the forests and will act naturally in his job. Fires set via arson is a different story altogether. You have asked me about forest fires and many people think we are the same as house fires, negligent fires, arson, and such. The act of burning is the same, but the motivation is different. We can talk about that another time.

The awe that onlookers see is such massive power, so close, so uncontrolled. When people watch this fire, their own feelings of inner power or powerlessness come out, whichever is strongest. Some fear it, some love it. Those who fear forest fires, fear their own emotions may become uncontrolled. Those who love it are not afraid of letting themselves go emotionally. Everyone has a desire to be powerful and uncontrolled. Some deny this, some know it and cannot express it, some do express it.

Thank you, forest fire.

Rocks On:
Graffiti—Ego Thoughts, Dark Action

At a somewhat secluded spot next to the Columbia River is a boat ramp. On either side of the sloped concrete are huge rocks defining the boat launching spot. Sometimes there is graffiti written on these gracious rocks. Many times there are questionable-minded boaters coming and going at this junction. I wondered what the rocks had to say about life.

Rocks, would you like to contribute to this conversation?

There are many sides to all issues. We present a side not generally requested. As we stand, we observe many things in a passive state. We don't flood, get excited, or have an abundance of energy. We just observe those that do.

This boat launch was ours years back. We gave way to allow people in. Excitement abounded at this time. People were thrilled with a boat launch. We observed and noted the people energy who loved this area. At night there was energy also, but not the joy as during the day. [At night] there was sneaky energy, plans being made, bottles thrown at us in ego play, destructive thoughts to impress other people. Our observation was that these people [wanting] to impress felt—the more destruction, the better. Writing on us was to gain validation from others. We don't know why this was so important. Feeling this ego energy was darker than the joy energy.

When the wind blows, it feels good. The wind connects the energy of the trees, rocks, sand, water as a unit. We are in a joyous symphony.

Thank you rock.

Columbia River On:
Life Isn't Just About Humans

As you know by now, many valued conversations were with the Columbia River and her inhabitants. Here are a few more significant and insightful chats with the River.

It is our collective path that we all have agreed to take. In this path are many learnings, growth, changes. We, the rivers, are changing as well as you humans. This isn't just about you.

Do you, the rivers/oceans, feel a change?

Of course. We swell, we retard, we get fuller, we wane. There is much more activities in our molecules—more excitement. This leads to doing things we normally may not do. Before, we would be content to stay within our banks. Now, the excitement—the added activity—makes it so we need more physical room.

Why do you flood in certain areas and not other areas?

There is more excitement, more activity more of a buzzing in those areas.

Yeah, but maybe there is more excitement because you are flooding.

Again, this isn't just about humans. All life has life and the ability to get excited, to have emotion, to feel extra movement. Say, when the daisies get excited, even though you may not see any physical signs of this, it effects all around in a subtle way. Well, most all life around the daisies know it, as if the daisies were screaming about it. Humans think of this as subtle, as this energy is felt rather than seen, and human feeling level is not as prominent as their sight. So according to humans there is no additional energy, yet all around feels it strongly. [To humans] nothing is different. So, as far as flooding, humans are oblivious and shocked when it floods, but all else in the area was totally aware.

How can we be more aware?

[Be] like the daisies. Develop your sensitivity a mite higher. Many things in today's life are asking/helping you to do this. Many classes are offered, many meditation styles are being opened up. Go sit under a tree. Go tune into your dog. Go talk to the river. Allow yourself to these forms of insight and feelings.

Thank you river.

Columbia River On: Movement of the River Floor

When I went to talk to you earlier, the mighty Columbia, you were cleaner than normal. And, waves and movement were there without it being windy. I just wanted to know what you had to say.

Sometimes surface things move the top waters. And the top waters cleanse the top portion of the waters in that area. Things get pushed on banks, on shore, and it is a natural cleansing. The water is still as polluted as before. It just looks cleaner on the top. When are you going to clean my banks?

(Side passing the question...) Is there something happening underneath you? Is it different than other times in your life here on earth? Tell me what's going on, on your floor.

The floor does feel a vibration, a movement. This creates for much work to be done on the floor, as every movement disarranges how it was. [Just] like someone coming in and moving the furniture in your house. The floor begins to be not as solid and not as flat. So in that arrangement of new things, where rocks move, and things move and change on the floor, then it creates movement and change for all particles on the floor, which creates the change and movement of life near the floor. The change in the fish creates a change in the pattern of the water flow. It changes the way that the flow has been for quite some time. There is nothing good or bad about this, it's just a change and lots of work that we have to do. It's just something that is.

In the changes of the flow in the river, it changes the banks of the river, it changes the people, and the structures, and the human life, and animals, and trees. In answer to your question, there is more rumbling underneath that shakes the floor of the river. These rumblings come from deep within. I speak not of just the Columbia River, but of many, if not all rivers in the world.

Different things [have] happened to rivers in the last 20 years, than [in] the last few hundred years. Rivers change course, go into different areas that it hasn't before. So many things have changed with the river, in so many aspects. And the future of the change is more rumbling. This is not a one time deal, it is an ongoing shift that creates movement of the floor of the rivers, due to what's beneath the floor of the river.

When it gets high enough to affect humans and they ask questions, it has already gone on for quite some time. The fish know, they live there. The algae knows, they live there. They have experienced this for quite some time. It is an ongoing change. I foresee more. What I don't foresee is how the top of the river actually affects humans. I see the floor of the river up to the middle of the river, as that is my base of interest. It does affect the top of the river and you would have to talk to another aspect to get more information. This [the deeper waters] is like my specialty.

What would be the outcome of this?

How humans are affected by our movement will determine the outcome. If humans tried to stop what's going on, changing the flow of the river, trying to control it, it would be much more devastation than if they just allowed us to be. We cannot stop what we are doing. We do not want to stop what we are doing. It is a process. And it is a fine process. There is nothing wrong with it. Humans seem to think there is something wrong with it, out of fear. So, in their fear, they hastily try to stop or control the river. It is a futile attempt.

I assume it is important to you that it is an *expensive* attempt, because you will not control the river. The river will do what the river is going to do. I don't foresee the outcome today. I don't care. There is extra movement. When more movement comes, we just deal with it. The most difficult part is that the humans try to stop it. If we had more people flowing to the banks of the river and honoring it and blessing it and kissing it and loving it, we could do our work in joy. We have people running to our banks in fear. Trying to stop us—don't do this. You're going to hurt us and we can't tell them otherwise—but *you* can. Teach this.

The question of when I was going to clean its banks bothered me for a few days. Finally, I took a couple garbage sacks down to the river and did some cleaning of the river's edge.

Columbia River On:
No Separation Between Water and Shore

Here is another wise perspective from the river.

There is peace in the river. In the winter time the river is not as wild and crazy as other times of the year. That's because there is peace, lack of energy in people. And the river is people in a different form. What you are learning has much to do with the rest of us. What we know is unity. What we know is that everything is us, that we are everything. There is no separation. There is no separation where the water meets the shore. There is no separation where the water surface meets the sky. It just changes form. How can you say that ice is different than steam, when ice melted becomes liquid, liquid melted becomes steam. Ice and steam are the same thing only in another form. That is how it is with all things. And of course your observations will directly reflect your inner thoughts and feelings.

What this whole ball game is about in communicating with everything, is you are getting in touch with you. Everything that is said out there is what is said inside you. Because there is no difference where the water meets the shore, the shore meets the brush, the brush meets the pavement, the pavement meets the person which is you. There is no difference. You are the water, the water is you.

Okay river, then tell me how do I get to that point of unity, that point of really knowing that oneness?

Chipping away at old thoughts and old beliefs and being rational and learning rational ideas and thoughts will eventually enable you to feel those rational thoughts of unity. In other words, once you know that, in a logical sense, you are one with the river because it has been explained to you up-teen times, then you can spout it off in your dealings with other people. Yes, we are all one, although a part of you will not feel that. But the more you learn everything around that idea, that thought, that individual creation, the more you will understand and feel your unity with everything else.

So the path you are on is, of course, the correct path. The path you are on is one that will eventually meet your needs in understanding unity. When a person wants to learn something, it is best to teach that which they want to learn as that will enable them to learn quicker and more thoroughly. So I encourage you.

The world wants to connect with God, and there are so many facets of that. When a person wants to connect back with their source, God, and feel at one with God, or at one with everything else, which is God also, then that is a goal that every human being desires in one form or another. That is why there are marriages. That is why there are children. Other than to perpetuate the species, humans feel children are their connection to God.

You have chosen a different path, you have chosen a path of direct connection. When a part of you (collective) feels like what is really important in life is family, spouse, children, extended family, what a person is really wanting, and what is most important in life, is unity—that connection with God. And people get as close as they can on earth to God, through family. They have children, many children. They have a husband or a wife and if that doesn't get them close to God, then they get rid of the spouse and try another one. [They conclude] it is the spouse's fault. When one is clear about children and spouses, that the longing is for connection to God, then people will begin to come into themselves. Reach inside of themselves for that God connection and quit trying to put it on people, places, things 'out there' for them to feel that God connection.

Your job is to show people what it is that they really, really want in life [to connect with God]. And how do you do this? You know it first, intellectually. Second, experientially. You don't have to be there to teach. Pretty soon you will be one with God. And how a person gets there is of no matter. It doesn't matter how a person gets there. It only matters that they get there and they recognize what they are striving for. And all your religions and all your churches say they have the answers. And the answers are only if it feels right for you. Teach this.

Nevada River On:
Pretty is an Opinion

Driving north on I-395, the highway followed a river off to the east outside of Carson City, NV. Coming up from Bishop, California, it was time to take a little driving break. I stopped next to the river for some down time. In this, I was struck by the amount of fast flowing water in the river, but inches away was desert and dry areas obviously needing water! I had to retrieve my spiral notebook from the car and ask the river about life.

How come you are in such a hurry, river?

We have much energy flowing. This is conducive to fish who enjoy a fast flowing river. We represent the business in the calm of the desert. It is our desire to show the two totally different styles, wet and wild versus dry and quiet, side by side. Our water could take the dryness away, yet we choose to be separate, side by side.

What is it that you are trying to say in being side by side with your opposite?

Each being has a place and purpose on this earth.

You mean segregation is ok?

Look how we flow—quickly, yet in a peaceful manner. And look how quiet the hills and rocks and plants are.

Yes, looks like opposites to me.

To your eyes, maybe. We are united in the peace. Don't you feel the peace in the hillside?

Yes.

Don't you feel peace in the river?

Yes.

Why did you stop here?

Because of the contrast between you two. The wet river versus the dry hillside was intriguing.

And what have you noticed, now?

That you both represent peace and are part of the whole. It amazes me how you can be so full of wild water, yet five feet away is area needing water to grow and flourish.

Does it?

Well, I am used to the Pacific Northwest where it's green and lush where living things get plenty of water.

Is that the only way to be "pretty?"

I guess not. Your hillside rocks are unique, the foliage is unusual to me. And I look at all of this, plus the river, and it's beautiful here.

Thank you. We represent [that] there is beauty and peace in all things. If my waters watered the hillside, all the foliage you now see would die and different foliage would have to grow. This is not our intent. We honor the foliage that is here. And value it enough to let it be as it is. We [the river] meanders through, not as one trying to 'improve' anything, but enjoying it, just as you in your car are doing. Many species and beings can live together in harmony and peace and beauty, even if it looks 'opposite' to humans. That is all to say. Thank you for inquiring.

Thank you river and hillside and all.

Reno's River On:
A Place to Calm Gamblers

At one point I took a trip to Reno Nevada and spent some time writing. Not being much of a gambler, my off daytime was usually spent walking up and down the park next to the Truckee River near the hotel. One sunny day it seemed fitting to have a chat with the river.

Okay river, tell me what is it like being a river in Reno Nevada.

I am the calm where the casinos are the busy. I do my best to balance out the people who come to me. As the people who come to me are very one-sided due to the casinos. I try to balance them out.

Balance what?

I try to bring back to balance the four aspects: physical, mental, spiritual and emotional. In the physical, people come here [the banks of the river] to run. They come here to do things that are opposite of sitting and putting money into a machine, or gambling. Emotional: I give them inner peace where gambling gives them a false high. Spiritual: I give them just a taste of spirituality, although most do not realize it as such. Mental: a clearing of the mental thoughts. If someone spends enough time with me, I can balance them out from what they get with the gambling. Many of my people on the banks are visitors who come for the false high and on a day like today, where you get both me and the sun, we are able to balance people out more quickly, efficiently, or thoroughly.

I know the tourists value you, do the locals value you?

As with any other river going through a city, some do, some don't. Some see problems, some see God. I can only do my part in calming those who choose to be calm or those who are looking for ways to be calm.

So, do you get really full and then recede?

There is much snow on the mountains and the snow accumulates and comes down through the river. There is an abundance of energy when the snow enters the river. We welcome it, yet the molecules slow down and it gets colder here. And sometimes we do reach the banks but not very often. What you see here is low. We can reach much higher than this and will do so at some point.

What about fish? Do you have much fish here?

We do have fish. The more the snow comes into our waters, the more fish that come with the snow. And we bless the fisherman by periodically giving up our selves.

You have some beautiful trees on your banks and they are changing colors. Is there anything you trees would like to share? It is a gorgeous place here.

TREES: We, in conjunction with the sun and the river, provide solitude to those who are looking for solitude. We provide a connection to the other side and most people want that for only short periods of time. Then they either leave, fall asleep, or decide to do something 'productive'. We are here for as long as they choose. We get our water from the river so it is unlikely we along the river will die of thirst. As in the outskirts, our type of trees do not flourish. But since we have water from the river and from the city, we do flourish

Thank you, trees and river. I am familiar talking to you and talking to aspects of nature. What I am unfamiliar with is who I talked to earlier. (I had a conversation earlier with something who seemed to have a much higher energy level). So, can you help me, 1. To get back to that and, 2. Tell me what that was all about?

A focused effort will get you back to that. Just as you had difficulties talking to us at first, you have difficulties talking to a much more powerful source.

We are all aspects of God—the sun, the river, the bushes, the trees, the grass, the rocks. What you were talking to was the real thing. And that power you felt that you needed to run from will get more comfortable as time goes on. Right now, there may need to be a forcing to put yourself in a correct situation to be able to handle it to get used to that energy coming through. And then it will be as easy as pie—as easy as talking to us. It will flow, just as we [the river] flow. You will move fluently. Just as we travel down our path, this is your path.

So what is my path? Is it with you guys or is it with God?

There is no definite line. You keep wanting to know what this book will be about. What if there is no book? What if what you are doing, you do for you? What if there is no recognition for this? What if there is no financial reward for this? What if you find nobody wants to hear what you are channeling? How would you feel then? Would you still talk to us?

Yes. I'm not going to let this practice go because it feels so good for me to do it. Because when I talk to you, I am in a different space. And I am in a space I need to be in for my peace of mind. And if I quit talking to you altogether, I quit being in that space. And I will be in my illusionary world, and not reality. This is reality. So, I will have to say, even if nothing comes of it, I want to still continue with you and I want to experiment with this new energy I have found. Because I want to be in that space, because it feels good, because that's where I need to be to make the rest of my life worthwhile.

About that illusionary life I think is real. THIS, the conversations I have with you all, is what is real. This is what's important, this is what's good. I will do this for ME, not for anyone else. I am not doing it because I *have to* talk to all these various things. I can talk to the bushes, and I don't even know what species they are. And I can do that because I need to do that. It is who I am. It is what I want to be. I'm developing my communication with God. I'm still going to document it. Maybe I won't even write them down. Thanks for the conversation my friend.

Pacific Ocean On:
Viewing Me as You

Hello, vast ocean. You are so powerful, huge and magnificent. What words do you have for me and others today?

Look at me/us. I say me/us as I am one ocean. I am many faceted. As looking at me, you can see the breakers, the foam, the water, the power, the white, the green/blue. I am many things to many people. I am death and fear. I am majestic and calm. I am love. I am hate. I am what *you* decide to be or to see. Whatever you view in me, you view in you. I am you. That is what is meant by that saying. Not that human fingers or particles are the exact same makeup as I, but whatever you see in me is a reflection of what you see in you. And what is today's vision? [It is] …power, big, magnificent. If you were not these things, you could not see them in me. If you were fear, you would fear me—and some are/do.

So, the more positive you view everything out there, the more you see or are aware of your own beauty. And the more you see your own beauty, the more beautiful the planet is—including humans. You watched a dead person documentary last night [on TV] and it compelled you to see autopsies and the casualness of the workers [working with the dead bodies]. Begin to separate the body from the soul. What you saw were lifeless bodies, the vessel.

118

This is a grand lesson on dividing up the two forces, soul and body. See how the body is just a blob. And look at all the interpretations, beliefs, fears, limits, dislikes, and likes that you have placed on the body; on the one thing that carries *none* of that. The body is just a reflection manifested due to a soul/ego combination. The body states where the soul/ego connects in— merges. The soul is not human. The ego is not human. Both together create the human body. And in this body is where both reside for the time it is here. When the body dies, much ego dies with the body and the soul moves on. The soul needs the body to manifest on earth—to do soul work in body form, to merge with ego and balance out.

The most enlightened beings are the most balanced between soul and ego. Not those who have no ego, but those humans who value and appreciate both the soul and ego. As a human, ego is inherent. Trying to do away with ego is a fruitless journey. The body without ego is impossible. Yet you can value ego by laughing at its state instead of fearing. Such as, don't fear fear. Don't be angry at anger. Don't feel sad about sadness. Don't hate hatred. Just observe these states. Be there with all you've got to get to the other side—to get to love again. You are growing and learning and experiencing, and ego (fear, hatred, grief, sorrow, sadness, anger) will come up. Know that. Just allow it and do your best to get to the other side, to love, peace and joy. We love you. From the collective ocean to one body, we are all you see, you are all you see. We love all of you.

Pacific Ocean On: Power or Strength?

Ocean, you have such tremendous, yet subtle power. Talk to me about power.

First, thank you for asking. The power you perceive is your interpretation of who I am. To another I am play, to another I am fierce, to another I am gentle when compared to other ocean fronts. So, as everything you label, it is only you labeling you.

However, you want to know about my "power". I will comply. Power is in the eye of the beholder. My power or strength is a combination of all aspects in the ocean. The ocean doesn't necessarily have power, the ocean has energy. A collective energy that can be peaceful if you are a skin diver, deadly if you are in a storm. Our energy is also affected by the moon and the earth—as in quakes, volcanoes, shakes—by all beings residing in the ocean and also by humans. Our power, if you call it that, is the result of a collection of energies of all the above.

Power [is] an interesting word. I hadn't judged myself as powerful. That would be an ego-based observation. One that tells the observer or judger the lack of power she has or feels she has. She says I have power, then she says I have *more* power than she. She feels a less quantity of power than the ocean. And is she less powerful than the ocean? Let's examine that. Can I leave my shores and travel inward spontaneously? Not without cooperation and consideration for/from all my "parts". Can humans move anywhere spontaneously? Yes. They have built roads and cars and figured out how to travel anywhere easily.

Can I not care? No. All my parts care. Can a human? Yes. Free will even allows for apathy. Free will is very powerful, even more so than I. I have collective will. Humans have individual free will. They have collective will also, but some do not recognize it and feel very separate. It's okay, that's what builds cars and boats and planes. I have collective energy of many. Humans have energy of one. They think, feel, believe in that one energy. It's tremendous power. How one uses their energy or power is up to them. Thank you.

Tsunami of the Indian Ocean On:
Acceptance and Appreciation

I thought it was imperative to see what the massive killer wave of the Indian Ocean in December of 2004 had to say.

Tsunami, what would you like to bring to these insightful conversations? I could ask you a specific question like, "Why did you happen?", but I think just hearing what you have to say is most important.

I only have one thing to say—and that is, be kind to all your relatives and friends. They may be gone in an instant. You never know what is going to happen from one moment to the next. You don't know what will separate you with them. I aided in many separations. This moment is all you truly know you have. The kiss of death may be closer than you think. Just as my annihilation of humans, pets, and homes was only a moment away from reality. But did these people know it? Not at all. They didn't even believe it when I showed my face. They still felt such a thing could not happen to them. But they found out a bit too late that it *can* happen to them.

So, in the meantime, be certain to pay attention to this moment, to your family, your friends, your loved ones. Tell them you love them, as you may be parted with them in an instant. Treat each moment as the last. Appreciate, love, value who they are today. Don't worry about tomorrow. Tomorrow will come soon enough. Hopefully you will still be with your loved ones, but it's possible you may not be. I know I can say other things about why, how, the earth's floor, and such, but it really doesn't matter so much as to why I was there. Take my appearance as your opportunity to appreciate all that is around you, including yourself. In the end, that is all you have anyway. It will set the stage for a peaceful transition to the afterlife.

If you go [die] and you are not at peace at the moment of death, there will be a tougher transition. Not through any judgment, but solely through your own concerns. "I didn't do this", "I should have been nicer to my wife", "I don't want to go yet, I still have things to accomplish". In this mindset, you will fight the transition. And that makes it a bit harder, as you will have to travel from "no" to "yes". Or from "stop this" to acceptance. If you live with acceptance today, when you go, you will transit easier as you won't have to go through the initial fight or resistance of your death. Make a decision right now to be at peace. If you need, you can sit down and write those things you want to accomplish before you die. Then see if they truly need to be done. Eliminate them one by one until only the top one or two things are left. Then reevaluate those two and see if they truly need to be accomplished. What you will be left with is self, family, friends, people, life, nature. Be with them now, in all your mind, in all your being, in all your soul and attention. Just be with them and feel the peace within yourself. Life truly *is* good. Feel that. Just know that at any moment you or your loved one may end their life on this earth as you know it. And that this is okay. Be at peace now.

Thank you so much, tsunami. I didn't know you were going to go there! Very good advice.

Wind On:
Impact of High Winds

Today the Columbia River is high, the winds are strong. Tell me wind, what about hurricanes?

As you have noticed, wind brings energy, demands attention. One cannot ignore high winds. Wind has a thrill attached with it. Winds create people to breathe deeper. In doing that, many things occur.

a. Energy level increases.

b. Smells are brought into human system which reacts in specific ways— unconscious mostly.

c. Human aliveness, noticing expectations, fear, joy, anger—the emotions are heightened. A natural high or low, whichever emotion is being felt at the time.

Humans need to wake up to the fact that we [wind] can destroy you in a moment. Denial and lack of respect of our power is too common. Even with notice, the people in a hurricane's path who choose to stay can perish. Is it denial or unconscious death urge? You can use a hurricane as a tool to see how much denial one is in. How much denial will you stay in? This is similar to beliefs, knowings, truths. You can't discuss this with anyone not believing in it. They are in denial of both. They need to wake up. Wake up to truths. Wake up to reality. Wake up to self and God. Anyone trying to bring people out of denial into truth is labeled a troublemaker, an alarmist, crazy, or worthless. The ones with high self-worth are the ones saying truths. If they could be beaten down, they would have been by now.

Wind On: Making the River Dance

At the time of this chat, I was living near the second wind surfing capital of the world, the Columbia River Gorge. I didn't realize that wind and river and energy had such personalities. Maybe they are as alive as people? Today, the wind told me ...

I like to play with the river. I make it go so fast. And the river jumps with joy when I do that. You can see that. Humans call it white caps. It's the river jumping with joy because the river loves the wind. When one physically touches and affects the other, the wind touching the river creates a union that is different than the wind above the river (like in not touching). So the union, created by the physical touch of the wind and the river, is more of a joyful union. It is the energies of both, come together in bliss and fun and play. And when that happens, all surround jump for joy. The river jumps for joy at the aid of the wind.

The wind surfers got the right idea because the best time to wind surf is when the river jumps for joy. And that creates joy in people. So what you call "board heads" are not druggies, not drunks, not weirdos. Board heads have already learned the joy in the communion of water, wind, themselves, and their boards. And that is not anything others have not experienced, but the ones that have experienced it may not have really put it into words.

Teach people that being next to the water, or next to any form of nature, that they can see things in a different perspective. You just saw things in a perspective of the wind and the river that you never thought of before. The low self-worth [person] doesn't want to rock the boat as someone may tell them they are crazy. They are the sane ones, the denials are the crazy ones!

Even if it isn't blowing strongly, the wind is still there. Even when I am not wild and crazy, and have ample energy to make the river dance; there is a subtleness about me. I am multipurpose, multidimensional. I can bring different feelings to people at different times. Of course, everyone can feel how they want to feel, but my presence will help their moods—to feel a specific way. The wind, lots of me, builds excitement in people. They feel the wind, they think something will happen. It's like the horse who is ready to run or ready to investigate. The wind bring smells, and animals naturally pick up on this and follow the smells that interest them. Dogs do this, horses do this, or they run from them, or they are curious. When the wind blows highly, the same instinctual feeling comes to humans; an energy that they don't know what to do with. They definitely will feel the energy of the wind. Dogs and horses will react to it, people will react to it, but not in a direct manner. They will not act on the wind, they will just act. When I am quiet, I am still here. Wind is nothing more than air in its movement. And as you know, the air is still around you at all times. It has a calming effect. The more breezy [I am], the more excited a person will get.

Thank you, Madam Wind.

Cold, the Temperature, On: Non-judgment

Ok, I'd like to speak with another aspect of nature or whoever wants to talk to me.

Hello, I am cold.

Oh my! I'm speaking to the temperature?

To the state of the air in your atmosphere that you now consider as "cold". Sometimes it's hot, sometimes breezy, sometimes stagnant, sometimes fresh and clean.

Ok cold, what would you like to share? Just a second...are you wind? Are you air? How can you be cold?

I am the temperature of the air.

Today you are the cold that is in the air, huh?

Yes, I am the chill part of the air.

Ok, what would you like to share today, cold?

Today I am cold. Sometimes I am warm. Neither state is good or bad, both are positive. Both temperatures have good and bad factors, depending upon

126

how you view them and the standards you apply. You will hear people talk about the sun, the warmth and the desirability of warm weather. Warm weather is most conducive to human body temperature. However, the human only views temperature by his standards, needs, comfort. This is extremely narrow-minded. Let me list all the benefits of cold.

Please do.

Cold makes humans appreciate warmth. Cold perpetuates the cycle of life. Cold loves grass, earth and nature, as nature loves cold. Do the tree branches shrivel during winter time?

No.

Tree branches still reach upwards in an unclothed way, ready for cold to permeate its body, welcoming it, including the cold wind. Cold does not make the tree shrivel and die, but enhances it, making it stronger.

Thank you very much cold.

Moon On:
Human Spirit Chats

I got information one night while driving, but wasn't sure where it was coming from.

Is there an aspect of nature speaking to me—the moon? Moon, where are you in these amazing insights I've been getting from other beings?

If you look at me, I represent the spirit world. I represent the beings that are human and non-human alike. They are energy and this [moon] is a form of nature. It just is not a [energy] form that the human recognizes [as such]. And when you talk to me, the moon, you are speaking with a link to spirits, ghosts, humans passing over—any aspect of the other side that can relate [not only] on an animal/vegetable/mineral basis, but on a human basis. And there will be times where you will need human to human information for your journey and the journey with others you share these insights with.

Moon On: Night in Shining Armor

You are a crescent moon, talk to me.

Transition stage [for you] is not the best time to get quality work.

Me? What am I transiting to?

128

A higher level. You will be able to communicate with me and with other beings more.

Will I be able to talk with God?

There are many levels of god. If that is the term you want to use, that is fine with us. There are many levels of god.

What level am I talking to?

In your deserve-ability it would not be possible for you to say that you spoke to God and that God spoke to you in a convincing manner to others. You may say you spoke to angels, or to me [the moon], or to whatever you feel you are most comfortable speaking to. It's all up to you. Any time you speak with god, you speak to the highest level that you can, in your particular mindset. So, you will always be talking to the highest god that you can, that is possible for you. When you go higher, you will talk to a higher god. We don't care what you call it, god is fine. Others might [care] because they have some preconceived notion what god is to them. And your god may not be their god. If there is another appropriate word, it would be "angel". You may speak with an angel, but just know that your angel is a direct link to god, to the ultimate highest power.

Angel is an okay word, but how about just 'moon'?

I watch over you, even in the daylight. Even when you cannot see me, I am there for you. I follow you around. I am your "night" in shining armor. I am the one who cares for you and protects you. I am your angel.

So, do you have many people you are angels with?

What you see is yours. I want you to feel the relationship between you and me. If I told you I had many that I watched over, you would not feel special. So, for your benefit, I am the only one for you. When you started out talking to god [years ago], you saw me [the moon] and I was god to you. And there was no more accurate statement. You cried to me, you asked for help, I cried for you, because it was wondrous to feel emotion again. And I honor you for that, for having emotion and for expressing it, because it enables me to feel it, through you. And emotion is what sets you apart from other living forms on earth. It sets you apart from other people, also, because your emotions are different than other people's emotions.

Thank you moon.

Moon On: The Origins of Prejudice

Moon, I don't feel qualified to hear you and all your deepness, your wisdom. I'm afraid that my ability isn't that great to present you in the most honored, respected manner you are and deserve.

Want to try?

Yes.

There is one thing I know you can hear from me. Look at the moon. Really look at it. What do you see?

I see magnificence, grandiose, perfection.

Well, this is how we see you humans. Did you know that the moon has many "imperfections" in its surface—like crevasses, craters, etc.? If one was judging that the best moon was perfectly smooth, then I am imperfect. Perfection is not having standards to live up to. Perfection is total love for who one is, knowing that each crevasse and mountain is perfect. It cannot be any other way. Look at people who have standards that others—or self—must live up to. Who in the world came up with perfection being a [certain way, such as a] smooth surface? Someone who did not see the perfection in themselves, they labeled some part of themselves as imperfect and decided they needed to get "better". Why did they initially label themselves as imperfect?

I don't know, why?

Many stories have been told as to why/how this began—from the eating of the forbidden fruit, to the veil of forgetfulness, and all in between. The most important factor is that you have concluded that you are imperfect. After you have labeled yourself as imperfect, you then, using your mirror theory, you see imperfection in others. (The mirror theory is that whatever you see outside of yourself is only a mirror of that which is within you.) This is how prejudices are started, by feeling imperfect, by labeling others as imperfect, then having to justify this belief or thought. So one quickly seeks out the most obvious rationalization. That is, if someone looks different, acts different, speaks different, that is why they are imperfect. You then conclude that you must be okay, but the other person is imperfect because they are different than you. However, the whole time a part of you believes you are imperfect and to counter that belief you toss your imperfections onto another to falsely hide your own. "He is imperfect because he is unlike me". Wallah—prejudice.

Now, let me get this straight. Prejudice starts with that tiny but huge feeling or belief that I am imperfect? Because I am imperfect, my ego doesn't want to admit this so the ego sets out to hide my imperfections, and to convince myself that I am perfect. And all others—which is anyone outside of self not just like me—are those that are imperfect? And the more different they are to me, the more prominent the "imperfections" as I see it, and the stronger the prejudice? Am I getting it?

Yes, go on.

But the bottom line, the core decision here is that I, at one time, took on the belief that I am imperfect. Now, why did I do that?

Not through will, but through a factor of being human which we will not go into at this time. Just suffice to say that being human at your stage of evolution it was/is essential to harbor that belief, to accomplish what you set out to do. And the more obvious the differences between people, the more likely one is to label those differences as imperfections, and therefore "bad." Language is another obvious difference, as is clothing and hearing/understanding/communicating, [plus] cultural ways and means.

So, If we cannot change the feeling/belief of imperfections in ourselves, what can we do to counteract this belief?

Know this story. Know the core, the root. Realize this as a means to fight this belief.

Will we ever get to believe other than that we are imperfect?

Not at this time. When you as a race evolves higher, then this belief will dissipate. Today, do the best you can and focus on love. Know this belief is false.

Does that mean we are perfect?

Of course, all of life is perfect, "flaws" and all.

Thank you so much, moon. You are truly magnificent! And perfect just as you are.

As are you, my friend.

Mother Earth On:
Collective Thought

Okay, Mother Earth, what is going on? Is there a quickening—an acceleration of life's happenings? Is anything happening in the world and on the earth that is unusual, or are these things normal and we just have higher technology to detect them?

In the center of the earth is what you may consider a ball. This ball is the ball of thought—the ball of collective thought of all humans on earth. This ball of thought manifests itself on the surface of the earth and materializes to create life as you know it right now. All of what you see out there on earth, and in the news, and everywhere on this planet, has this base in the thoughts of humans—which is collected and held in the center of the earth, Mother Earth, who is I. I can only produce/materialize the thought that is of the collective consciousness.

Interesting take, any other words for us?

Just one—what you do with your lives in regards to the earth is crucial in unity, in survival of all species, in enlightenment of humans. Be aware of your earthly surroundings. Appreciate us in all our grandeur. Value us so much you do not want to damage us or litter. This will say a lot about you individually. And each aspect of nature will smile upon you, knowing you know us, value us, and have gratitude for us.

I'd like to ask you, Mother Earth, how can we best help you?

What I have found is that humans have not much self-confidence. If they only knew and could feel how important they are to every being on this earth, then they would straighten up their act and begin to fly right *for the highest good of all.* That means for all of us. We all are one, and if humans cannot feel that, then let us tell you, "don't do it for yourself or for the unity, do it for us, for the animals, for the plants, for all consciousness." If that is what it takes to get you motivated, fine.

What do we need to do?

Simple things, like doing what you wish everyone would do. You see people litter and you hate it, then you turn around and throw something on the ground. Take care of your own. Teach your children by your actions. You do this anyway, just make it conscious and see that your children are following your [exemplary] lead. Be the person you want them to be. Take action, no matter how much energy and time it takes. Get into the habit and recycle. Divide your garbage and dispose of it for the highest good.

Care for your land as you care for your yard. There are many gorgeous yards out there, yet the city streets are filled with trash. Pick up a couple items today and carry them to the garbage can. Think globally. [Ask] how is what I am doing affecting others, all others, not just humans? How is that trash affecting the city, the wild life?

Thank you, Mother Earth.

Nature On:
Volunteering to Die

One day I had a wonderful chat with something. I believe it to be collective nature. I was caught with my notebook down so there was no record of these insights. I didn't want to paraphrase this great chat, so I went out the following day for a repeat conversation so I could write it down, word for word. **Note:** *This chat was years prior to the horrific tsunamis that have hit the earth's shores. Those disasters come to mind when I read this chat now.*

So Nature, say what you said yesterday so I can get it in writing.

The draw is the wind, the water, the sun, and nature. As you know, these factors draw in people wanting to relax, come away from city and/or stress. These factors bring people in hoards. Why? People are drawn to these aspects of nature. People are drawn to the natural earth because deep down all humans know we are one. Animals do so too, yet they do not deny this. The drive back to unity, oneness gets stronger all the time. It is our birthright. Out of nature you are born, created, and the drive back to your creator is strong.

The natural disasters in the world are not the sun or nature getting mad, as nature does not judge. People are drawn to areas of future disaster if their ending is near. A call has been placed for anyone desiring to go on [die] and

134

nature observes these callings, obliging in ways not rationally possible. Such "volunteer death" is a response to a call of restructuring the earth. Not all will perish. Some will retire to other realms, some will stay as angels and spirits helping animals and humans. Some will be no longer, at their choice. People killed by humans have also agreed to this. The killers are responding to their darkest side as both light and dark are apparent. The two extremes, the two opposite choices are driving humans. Free will determines which will prevail and act out.

Nature On: Want Nothing

Since I was able to connect with just general nature (a profound idea!), I had several insightful conversations with this source. Here is one of those chats.

Good morning nature. What's special?

For you to be here and help us with getting our message out.

I'm here for you. I have put myself in god's hands and...

No, you haven't. You are again doing what you feel will get you what you want by saying you give up, [yet] I feel no resignation on your part.

How do I truly resign my will, then?

Live in the moment—no future, no past. Start by thinking only of today. People ask about tomorrow. Don't speculate. They ask about yesterday. Don't rehash. Trust.

And more? I want specifics, please.

Want nothing. Want what you have. Do this. Look at everything in your life today—everything. And pretend that all of this was once your goal and you have reached it. This includes the [looks of your] body, the messy house. Understand to its fullest extent that you have finally got what you have been dreaming/thinking about. Look at your people frustrations and act as if they are you, only. There is no one else, only mirrors of you.

Including nature?

How you perceive nature is how you perceive yourself. Those fisherman out there (on a boat in the river), you perceive to be in peace. That is because you are in peace at this moment. If you decided the fisherman were unhappy, frustrated, then that would be due to your projection of what is inside of you.

135

Always pretend today is your birthday. Appreciate it all. Your life will go much smoother. Don't hang onto ego-driven desires. Learn to know who you are, what you want in life, see the beauty, and go for the gold that life has to offer. That which surrounds you will comply with this way of being.

Thank you.

CHATS WITH "JESSUP" AND THE HIGHER PLANE

This chapter is a conglomeration of chats I've had with my lifelong friend, Jessup. I am not exactly sure who Jessup is, maybe he is a group of entities from another dimension, maybe he is my higher self, maybe he is a spiritual guide, maybe Jessup represents universal intelligence, or maybe Jessup is simply a figment of my subconscious mind. Whoever Jessup is, he always brings in wonderful information from "somewhere." The most important factor is that we are open enough to hear and absorb his unique messages.

Jessup On:
The Veil of Forgetfulness

I would like to identify you. Who are you? What do you consider yourself? And do you have a name?

I am Jessup. I am the one who has been with you for so long on your journey. I am what you would call an angel, I guess. One who helps and guides you along in your journey of self-discovery and enlightenment. Names are not specifically correct, as I am more than one being as you know it. I am more the "spokes-angel" for many beings. I have been programmed—wrong word, schooled—in connecting with humans. I have to lower my vibration level to get this information to you. Other beings don't have that skill, or care to. They work through me. And I get info to you and you get it out to others in your dimension, other humans as you know them, others with your same vibration level, or similar. Are you with me? I sense some hesitancy.

Only that I may get distracted and lose my train of thought.

That is your choice.

I guess I can put aside all other things and not allow distractions, huh?

That is part of this discipline.

Okay, you have ten minutes. I will commit to not being distracted for ten minutes. That's all I can commit to right at this minute.

138

Good enough. The question is about equality. When there were humans in the first days of human existence, all were equal in all aspects. Humans were like us, all loving, all knowing, all connected. Then it was decided to have the veil of forgetfulness cover all humans so God could experience his creation. In this forgetting of who and what they were, humans inherently assumed that they were "less than." Without that knowledge and feeling of connectedness, a part of each human knew there was something missing inside. When the veil was draped on you, and your knowledge and soul connection was hampered, there was a vein of misunderstanding. All of a sudden you did not know who you were, where you were going, or why you came here. This meant the veil worked perfectly, as a child who knows not how to walk, but has the inherent instinct to do so through no logical conclusion. The child does not understand why he wants to walk, he just wants to, and will do so regardless of his ability. It is programmed in each child to *want* to walk. This is called evolution. Every human has this inherent within him. Every human wants to remember what he once knew. The veil is more like a blanket as there is no seeing through it. There is only a tug of war to get the blanket off. Every human will achieve that goal. As every child will one day walk.

It is not possible for a person to *not* achieve the goal of remembering who they are, feeling that connection, and being at one with all others. As every child will learn to walk in his own time, every human will evolve in his own time. Some will take 500 lifetimes, some will take two. In this age of acceleration, the urgency of evolving is known at some level in each human. There is a push in the universe for those who are to evolve to do so; and those that will not evolve will go the opposite way. The earth will soon begin anew. The evolved beings will inherit the earth. The weak as some say. Weak only in that evolved beings do not choose to fight over anything. They create. If things are not at their liking, they create another situation where it is. One that is better, more to their liking. Evolved beings do not hold on to fear. They let go. Is my time up?

Okay Jessup that was thirteen minutes. You just gave an abundance of great information, I didn't know I could get that! So, I thank you. You put it in a grand perspective. I have to rest now.

Jessup On: Connecting Back to God

At one time I did some hard thinking about how life works and was explaining it to further clarify my learnings. At that time, Jessup had something to say.

I want to see what you [collective] do with it [free will], because I believe that you will want to come back to me. But in your doing so, you will experience every emotion there ever is and I want to feel it. So I'm going to feel all those emotions through you. And I want to be part of your path in coming back to me. On your journey back to me, I am able to experience everything, and that's what I want. I want to experience everything. And on your journey back to me, we both will experience everything. And you have free will. I want to see where it will take you. I want to see how you use your free will. And maybe next time when I create, I will create a little differently. I want to see how this one works out. [With] free will you can do anything you want. I want to see what happens.

What is happening now is you are destroying your world. Too bad, it is a grand world. So, [as] every one of you [comes] closer to coming back to me, you will feel more like me, until you feel at one with me. So in your journey back to me, the closer you get to me, the more spontaneous, the more play, the more fun, the more you will go with your gut feelings. Because you will know that that is me talking to you. The closer you get to me, the more willing you are of honoring the god part of yourself.

Jessup On: Starving People

Jessup, I'd like to understand further about why people choose to reincarnate directly into extremely difficult circumstances. My understanding is that some souls choose to be born into countries where children are starving in those countries, and to eventually succumb to starvation itself. Is the reason they do that to experience all the struggles and hardship and devastation of dying of starvation? Is that what they need to learn at this particular time? It doesn't sound plausible. I am getting confused. So can you explain it to me further?

As with every answer there are aspects of those answers that are understandable [to you]. It's too complex to be able to tell you the whole story in a nice succinct little package. So when you get different answers for the same question, the answers are all part of the big picture. What is difficult to explain to you is how the complete big picture works. So we took out parts of the big picture that you can understand and tell you that. So you can at least see that part of the picture.

As you know and understand that part, we can add another part. The ultimate goal is to finally get the big picture to you so you can see it in our light, how we see it. So, in your answer about starving people, there is an aspect that is happening. The soul doesn't *need* to experience anything, the soul *wants* to experience all things. When the children are born [into these situations], they are born through a decision, whether conscious or unconscious, of the mother and father. That decision is put into the brain of both parties by the help of the soul of the child. The child wants to experience this. When that child is [in] soul [form]—which is only a higher percentage of knowledge that it is god—the child has many options. Quite often the child would come into the world for the parents or the siblings. If the child dies very young, the soul of that child is put to service. The soul doesn't necessarily come to experience that life starving to death. It came to provide experiences for others, parents, siblings, other people in the tribe.

Okay, when you get all these people in this tribe and they all are starving and that is all that is happening, it doesn't seem to me there is much to learn. You are in survival mode, then you die. You have babies, then they die. What is the benefit of even have one more to be born and die?

Do you think that your life is the only way one can learn? Is your lifestyle the only one who can grow and evolve? These people are doing exactly what you are doing only in another way. Because death means something different to your society, it does not mean that these people are not learning anything, and not growing or evolving. They are doing it in another manner. And every society, every lifestyle, is completely valid in their evolutionary process. The soul grows.

Again, I want to caution you that not all societies believe the way your society believes. So to see other people, other societies, and take that information and pictures and interpret it into *your* society rules, then you see things in a very one-sided way. If you step up one level and observe without judgment, then you will just look at what is happening and not feel it.

Observation is a wonderful thing. Starving kids in New Guinea [or wherever] are just that. They are starving kids in New Guinea. That's not right or wrong. It just is. I have given them tools. Everyone has given them tools to get out of their pattern. And as of yet they are not utilizing those tools. Maybe they don't want to. Maybe this is such a grand growing circumstance that they want to continue this. Let me stretch your imagination a little bit. Maybe these souls come into these starving kids' bodies for the highest accelerated growth that they could ever achieve. My point is your judging that this is wrong and that these people don't want to be there. So that is one aspect of it. Another aspect is a prism.

There are so many aspects to every incident, every lifestyle, every thing, that it is very difficult for me to impart all of that wisdom on you. Each time you have a question, come ask and I will answer. And this answer may be in a different prism than the last answer. Rarely will I give you the same answer twice. Because you already heard the answer in prism A, and you don't need me to repeat it. And if you ask the same question, you haven't quite gotten it. Let me answer you in prism B and see if you get that. When you get to prism X then maybe you will say, "Oh, I understand, now. Now, all of these things make sense. I thought I was getting different answers all along. Now I see that every answer I got when I asked the question was right. It just was from another angle." We will try anything to teach you to bring that memory back so you know. Because that is what you want to do, what you are here for. And we love you grandly and we will give you any information that we can. So please keep asking, even if it's the same question over and over again. Keep asking, and finally you will say, "Oh, I got it, now."

Thank you so much.

Jessup On: Upcoming Earth Changes

It is my pleasure to introduce a new thought into you. One to contemplate, swish around in your mouth as a fine wine. One to smell the cork and taste the excitement of the flavor, the new flavor. A new world is upon us now. There has been a shift of magnitude proportions. Each and every member of the human race feels this to some degree.

How do we feel this?

Many sense discomfort as their situation, their being, has shifted. Those based primarily in fear will react in this fear manner. Many new disasters and human fear actions will continue to take place. I urge you all—first you and then to everyone—to get the word out. Just know this shift has now happened and you will be affected. How, is up to you. If you have sufficient love and trust (which is the same thing, the same base), you will exercise that more. Detach from the fears of others. Assist with "fear bandages" (masking the fears on the surface), and remind them that this fear is temporary and will heal soon. Encourage laughter, fun, play, community. This will alleviate some fears, and heal some old wounds; which is essential to your (collective) growth, as to yours, too. [It will] heal wounds of family and old friends. [Make sure] no hard feelings are lingering, as the time is near when old either gets healed or the scar deepens. And this is not good for where all are going, including you.

Where are we going? And what's in store?

The line has been drawn in the sand. Humans, the majority, have crossed this line into a new dimension. This is good news for us, but slight disarray for you. Just love through it and trust. Many things will happen quickly now.

You have said these things for a long time.

But now is when the majority have shifted. Before, it hadn't completed the shift.

What things can we expect?

Your stock market is an example of the disarray that is within people. Up and down, down and up. More murders, more mass murders, more people leaving the planct. Their time to leave is imminent now. They do not choose to see this [change] through. Do not fault them if they choose suicide or disease. Those in their midst will take a lesson on love and letting go. Detachment will be a hard lesson for some, but it will prove to be for the highest good of all. Practice love in a detached manner. That is the highest love.

How long is this transition?

Years, many years, yet, no time at all. Just know the preparation was successful and many have reached a higher thought of love on this plane, as have you.

Thank you. Yes, I think I have.

Our love goes out to every one of you, even to those who do not read this. Just know that they, too, are part of this program, this transition. Do not damage those who do not think like you. Just know some are in fear and reacting to this shift in a difficult manner.

What about those seemingly in transition? Should they grab and hold on to security, the past? Or should they let go and grasp the new?

One would seem as though grabbing the past is security, but it is not. Grab the trust and love within, with us, with that in which is highest in your thoughts. We will assist you in the transition, but you must ask us. We encourage partnerships here, but not what you think. We encourage the God-self partnership. Thank you.

Oh, thank you.

EPILOGUE

These chats have been a significant part of my life. I honor all who have contributed. I hope these insights have encouraged you to know you are not alone and to eagerly continue the means to connection, happiness, and joy in your path to evolvement. Thank you for having the courage to read what our fellow beings have to say.

--Cynthia Attar

Profound Insights from Animals and Nature

INDEX

INSIGHT	SPOKEN BY	PAGE NO.
Getting Along with My Herd Family	Satchmo, the Donkey	52
God in a Shoe Box	Baby Squirrel	71
Graffiti—Ego Thoughts, Dark Action	Rocks	107
Honoring Us or Selfish Greed?	Salmon Fish	91
Human Development Verses Happiness	City Tree	100
Human Spirit Chats	Moon	128
I Want a Horse Buddy!	Neighbor Horse	61
Impact of High Winds	Wind	123
Inner Power	Featherless Bird	83
Joy of Playing	Neighborhood Dog	38
Laughter and Mule Tricks	Sally, the Mule	59
Let's Make a Deal	Sugar Ants	68
Life Can Be Fun!	Cat	17
Life Isn't Just About Humans	Columbia River	108
Making the River Dance	Wind	124
Movement of the River Floor	Columbia River	109
Night in Shining Armor	Moon	128
No Separation Between Water and Shore	Columbia River	111
Non-Judgment	Cold, the Temperature	126
Older Horses as Burdens	Candy, the Arabian Mare	51
Oneness	Maple Tree	98
Origins of Prejudice	Moon	130
People Abusing Animals	Dicky Doo, the Xolo Dog	53
Playing Well with Others	Satchmo, the Donkey	53
Power or Strength?	Pacific Ocean	119
Pretty is an Opinion	Nevada River	113
Pride On A Job Well Done	Shetland Pony	6
Quit Being so Rigid, Bend a Little!	Bamboo	103
Rejuvenation Of Life	Zip & Candy, the Aging Horses	47

INSIGHT	SPOKEN BY	PAGE NO.
Silent Royalty	Rita, the Guinea Pig	26
Soaring to Bless the Earth	Raven	87
Starving People	Jessup, the Spiritual Guide	140
Territoriality	Rattlesnake	93
The Historic Value of Mules to Humans	Sally, the Mule	59
The Importance of Smelling & Barking	Cheyenne, the German Shepherd Dog	34
The Inevitable Destruction of Earth	Spokesdog	40
The Urgency to Nest	Bird	85
Unity in Flying in Flocks	Canadian Ducks	77
Upcoming Earth Changes	Jessup, the Spiritual Guide	142
Veil of Forgetfulness	Jessup, the Spiritual Guide	138
Viewing Me as You	Pacific Ocean	118
Volunteering to Die	Nature	134
Walk-in to a Cat Body	Dicky Doo, the Xolo Dog	31
Want Nothing	Nature	135

www.ingramcontent.com/pod-product-compliance
Lightning Source LLC
Chambersburg PA
CBHW030018290326
41934CB00005B/385